HOW TO PROFIT
FROM YOUR
ARTS AND CRAFTS

HOW TO PROFIT FROM YOUR ARTS AND CRAFTS

Albert Lee
and Carol Allman Lee

David McKay Company, Inc.

New York

ACKNOWLEDGMENTS

This book was made possible through the diligent efforts of many people, too many to name and thank here. But we would like to give special acknowledgement to our project assistants: Mary Mulvey, Ginger Przybys, Florence Schumacher, and Nancy Emmert.

Library of Congress Cataloging in Publication Data

Lee, Albert, 1942-
   How to profit from your arts and crafts.

   Includes index.
    1. Handicraft—Marketing.   I. Lee, Carol Allman, joint author. II. Title.
HD2341.L4   658.89′7455   78-1507
ISBN 0-679-50831-7
ISBN 0-679-50868-6 pbk.

10 9 8 7 6 5 4 3 2 1

MANUFACTURED IN THE UNITED STATES OF AMERICA

Designed by Tere LoPrete

Contents

1. In Your Hands 1
2. Designs on Success 11
3. Pricing for Profits 21
4. Selling on Consignment 37
5. Everybody Loves a Fair 45
6. Marketing Techniques 63
7. From Post to Profits 73
8. Augmenting Your Crafts Income 99
9. Selling Yourself 118
10. The Paperwork 131
11. Cooperation Pays 160
  Listing of Crafts-Related Magazines 176
  INDEX 182

"If only you could tell them that living and spending isn't the same thing ... If only they were educated to live instead of earn and spend. They ought to sing in a mass and dance the old group dances and carve the stools they sit on and embroider their own emblems. And that's the only way to solve the industrial problem. Train the people to be able to live and live in handsomeness without need to spend."

D. H. LAWRENCE
Lady Chatterley's Lover

CHAPTER ONE

In Your Hands

Crafts are coming to life in America today. A revival—more like a renaissance—of interest in arts and crafts is enveloping the country. Major universities are establishing chairs in crafts, and curriculum offerings for continuing education programs are dominated by crafts classes. Museums that once shooed crafts peddlers off their property are now showing crafts works and selling handcrafts in their gift shops. Art fairs, regional shows, community exhibits, and shopping mall festivals crowd calendars everywhere. Even the government is promoting crafts. A dozen federal agencies fund crafts development programs both to inspire cottage industry and to perpetuate the traditional arts of a nation. And, most important, ordinary people are showing interest in buying and displaying crafts in their homes and offices.

Why all the interest? There are many reasons, but chief among them is that most Americans have been saturated with sameness. Although mass production has stamped out a materially better life for most of us, the inevitable byproduct has been depersonalization. Possessions, such as curios, teflon cookery, and photocopied paintings are like belly buttons—everyone has them, and one looks pretty much like another. Everywhere people now seek the unique items that give their homes and themselves a measure of individuality. Mass production has provided the leisure time for many to acquire tastes for the distinct design, texture, and color of an object.

A new and growing concern for our environment has also contributed significantly to the revitalization of crafts. More people have come to respect the value of hand labor and to mistrust the power-hungry machinery of our age. This concern is expressed in a strong back-to-nature movement, a return spiritually to lifestyles that were simpler and yet more environmentally sensitive. Traditional designs and the skills of an earlier age, such as candle making and leather working, are given new respect. The new environmentalists, with their adoration of plant life, have vastly increased the potter's and macrame craftsperson's market as well.

Some craftspeople see the boom as a potential bust for their business. As more people have the time and money to take up crafts, the hand skills lose status. After all, you can produce most of the crafts now being sold with inexpensive kits from your corner hobby store. Do-it-yourselfers and dabblers are popping up everywhere. This influx of leisure-time interest, however, can serve only to elevate the skilled craftsperson's work. Those who have attempted needlepoint or pottery as a hobby have enough knowledge to respect true crafts when they see them displayed. More fiddlers make Isaac Stern all the more sought after. Lay interest also opens up many new avenues of profit for the craftsperson—in teaching or selling designs for kits or manufacturing, for example. Ultimately, the more people who participate in and buy crafts and crafts materials, the better it will be for all of us.

Whether these new enthusiasts are moved by true aesthetics or simply a desire for novelty and escape from boredom is not the point. The salient point is they are indeed moved to quality and art. Lady Chatterley's dream is closer to reality. And your skills have never been better received.

But chances are you're not getting a significant piece of the market pie. Not yet, or you wouldn't be reading this book. Money, marketing, and business are seldom the drawing cards for newcomers to an art form. Most people take up crafts for relaxation or self-expression. The first creations are kept and prized or given to relatives and friends in ever-widening circles. This is followed by a few special orders from a friend-of-a-patron-friend or sales at the community art show or church bazaar. Satisfaction, accolades, money, and then comes the temptation to make your skill pay for more than the materials used.

Crafts can pay, yet most craftspeople never get beyond the dabbling stage. The vast majority remain moonlight artists and part-time practitioners. They may fantasize about fame and fortune, but few take the necessary steps to create a new reality. Thus they never realize the full potential of their work nor have the opportunity to refine their creations in the critical light of experience. Avocation never becomes vocation.

The obvious reason for this timidity is fear of "business." Few craftspeople, even those trained in their art form through four years of college, have any understanding of marketing or accounting practices. Creating with eye and hand is pleasant, but all of that asset–debit stuff is pure work. Worse, it's esoteric, and if done wrong, can lead to a business word that everyone understands: bankruptcy. According to the Small Business Administration, about 60 percent of all new enterprises go under the first year. Faced with such grim prospects, craftspeople generally feel no confidence in plunging in.

Yet success or failure rarely hinge on a craftsperson's business acumen. The most respected craftspeople, in fact, are those who do not make typical business compromises. These crafts artists refuse to impugn the integrity of their designs by using cheaper materials to cut costs. They do not sell their failures as "seconds." One macrame artist, striving for a specific color, throws out a large portion of the yarn she dyes until she has precisely the hues she envisioned. These are thoroughly unbusinesslike approaches, yet because these artists emphasize design, distinctness, and quality, they have become most successful.

You needn't be a businessperson to succeed, but you do have to know a little about business. Although only a small segment of the artist's time is spent away from the bench and in the books, it is important time, because this is where the cash flow is decided. You don't have to prostitute your skills or integrity, but you can't be sloppy about the business side either. If the thought of business turns you off, then just don't think about this time as business. Break it down into manageable parts that are less threatening.

Marketing, for example, is really only a high-sounding name for selling your crafts. And sales presentations mean little more than having a casual conversation with one person. In fact, no matter which marketing approach you favor—store consignment, chain buyer sales, wholesaling, agents, fairs, or direct mail—you will find that you never deal with more than one person at a time. If you are not put off by explaining your work to a casual acquaintance, then marketing and sales should not bother you.

Similarly, instead of thinking of shipping and receiving procedures, invoices, and the like, call it "mailing." All of us mail packages at holiday time. So what's the big deal? And as for the biggest bugaboo of all—bookkeeping—bear in mind that the books for a crafts business really aren't much more complicated than your family checkbook. When you get into the big dollars, then you can farm out those aspects of your business you are least proficient in (unless that happens to be your craft). Public accountants can do your taxes and your monthly bookkeeping for you. In most cases they will give you enough solid advice along with the work to more than justify their fees.

Actually, the toughest business considerations come at the very beginning of your decision to sell your crafts and infrequently whenever you decide to expand or radically change your offering. They are the design and pricing considerations. You have to do some sharp pencil work to decide what the real cost of materials and your time will be and how many less-obvious costs, such as breakage, taxes, and wholesale discounts must be included in your per-item price. The pricing stage is important to value-conscious shoppers, but not nearly so important as the design itself. Remember, you will not survive competing head-on with mass-producers. Unless your design sets itself apart from the stamped-out items on the shelves, unless it has an aesthetic or functional appeal unique to itself, there is no real market.

Like the other aspects of business, the decisions on salable designs and prices are not complicated. It is simply a matter of setting your ego aside and placing yourself in the buyer's head. Shop around. Find out what similar items are selling for in a number of different stores. Ask yourself if your design is different and even better than the herd. Answer yes, and you're in business.

All of this, of course, is oversimplification. This entire book and volumes like it devote themselves to giving you the skills summarized in the last few paragraphs. And although there is profit to be made at crafts, few people ever make a killing in this market. Outstanding craftspeople can earn a good living, but few will make their fortunes at it. A handful of master craftspeople have been known to earn $100,000 in a year. The majority, however, survive on a far more modest scale. Rags-to-riches stories are not common in any of the creative arts. Most performing artists teach dramatics. Painters do posters. Symphony orchestra musicians moonlight in disco dance bands. And novelists write advertising copy and cookbooks. The expressive arts are notoriously underpaid. They are inundated with amateurs willing to work for nothing just to become established, viewed, or published. While many crafts have a utilitarian function that other art media lack (a pot holds beans and a silver tea service serves), still, handcrafts are a long way from practical purchase necessities. No craftsperson can sell on purely pragmatic grounds. Crafts are luxuries that must, like most art objects, compete on aesthetic standards.

Yet money is not the measure in the expressive arts. "It's a trap," one craftsman told me. "You produce a piece with a mass-market appeal, and you become swamped with orders. Soon you're the prisoner of your product." This craftsman, like most expressive artists, limits his production of the highly salable items to have the time for creation and refinement of his art. In other words, the artist works for time more often than for money. The distinction between fine arts people, who work on one-of-a-kind pieces to express themselves, and craftspeople, who do quantity work to serve customers, is misleading. True artists in any medium work to express themselves, not to grow fat with profit. Not that there is any shame in making money or eating regularly, but for the expressive artist, there is no ultimate honor to it either.

This brings us quite naturally to your needs. A crafts business can work, but the overriding consideration is, can it work for you? There are many niches in the crafts industry. There is room for the college-trained artist and for the Appalachian welfare recipient who simply wants to earn enough money to get off the welfare roles. There is room for youthful expression and senior-citizen thoughtful precision. There are spaces for the counterculture craftsperson who hawks his or her wares on the street and for the designer consulting for corporate doodad manufacturers. There are spaces for artists and engineers, loners and promoters, urban intellectuals and down-home traditionalists. Yet in the great variation there are common requirements. You can find your niche, but you must also find out if you are going to be happy within it.

Doing a few pieces for friends at your leisure is a far cry from filling orders for your supper. The recreation of a hobby craft does not necessarily translate into a career of fun and games. One corporate executive, for example, chucked the "structured life" in favor of ceramics work at home. To his amazement, he found that his independent life was even more structured. There were no more three-hour lunches, no boondoggle business trips and cocktail parties—just long hours tied to his bench, far more than he ever had been to his desk. "After six months," he said, "I retired back to the corporate ranks." He did learn how to sell his crafts and now uses this knowledge as an extra source of income and pleasure, which is probably what he should have aimed for at the beginning.

Take stock in your lifestyle. How much money do you really need, for example, to be comfortable? New businesses seldom show a significant profit for the first year or two. You'll need money in savings to get by. But you will want to look toward a day when you can again enjoy your idea of comfort. It is one thing to say the material things don't mean much and you can get by with less. It's another thing to start looking at specifics. You mean I can't afford an evening out for poker? Home permanents instead of hairdressers? Beer instead of martinis? If you are starting from the bottom, it is more a question of water instead of beer, but whichever direction you are coming from, your creature comforts must be considered.

Some people cannot tolerate the insecurity of not knowing where their income will be coming from a year or two hence. Others start thinking about retirement benefits at age thirty. These people probably won't be comfortable in the tumultuous crafts business. The successful craftsperson often would be frustrated in the confinement of a regular job, not necessarily by the work load, but by the hierarchy which does things because "that's the way it's always been done" or "it is written in the company manual or organization chart." There are a good many self-employed people who could be more financially successful in the corporate world if only they could tolerate the regimentation.

A professional attitude toward one's work is another critical factor for the successful craftsperson. On the one hand, there must be a degree of detachment. Your creation cannot be looked upon as an extension of your personality any longer. It is one piece that must be considered from many different viewpoints. This detachment fosters an ability to be critical of the work without jeopardizing your ego. And criticism is a vital aspect of creative growth. On the opposite hand, you must have a good measure of self-confidence that may seem to border at times on conceit. Actually, it is a confidence not in the self, but in knowing that the work has merit. You must believe in your work if you are to sell it.

There are many other considerations of your own temperament and talents that you should work through before deciding on a radical change from part-time dabbler to working craftsperson. In general, you should take a hard look at your lifestyle. Ask yourself what aspects of what you are doing now are to your liking? What current hassles could you live without? And what will your life as a craftsperson really be like? Try to come as close to the experience as possible. Make not one or two copies of a design, but fifty, in a predetermined time to see how you hold up and tolerate repetition. Some gain skill through it and enjoy the pattern of activity. Others go bananas. And, above all, take stock in your personality and self-employment. There are two excellent books available that explore the profile of the independent businessperson. Peter Weaver wrote one about his own experience in the corporate world and his ultimate escape. The book is entitled *You, Inc.* (Dolphin-Doubleday) and is must reading. The second book is by psychiatrist David Viscott, *Feel Free* (Dell), and explores the opposition you can expect from friends and relatives when you decide to cut away from the pack. Neither one of these books appears in crafts business publishing lists, but they should.

One of the truly delightful aspects of the crafts world is that you can dabble in every aspect of it to decide what is most rewarding for you. We've all met teachers, lawyers, and engineers who, after going through the years of college courses, discovered, only after working in the field, that they did not enjoy their vocation. In crafts, you can taste before you buy. There is no need to decide today on either a career in crafts or nothing at all. You can experiment. Increase your crafts production for a period of time while it's still a hobby to see if the grind of production is for you. And if high production isn't your thing, you can do further experimentation into other crafts-earning methods. Try creating one-of-a-kind designs and selling them to crafts workers and industry or packaging them in kits. Write about your crafts instead of struggling with production. Teach for a while. Consider a syndicated column on crafts or possibly guest lecturing if you have a theatrical bent. You can even get into supplying materials to craftspeople to find out if your real satisfaction comes from associating with creative people rather than objects.

As you will see throughout this book, selling your skills as a craftsperson is easy and, at times, an enlivening experience. The markets are many and hungry for originality, quality, and utility, not only for your crafts, but for your insight and imagination. The most complicated ingredient is you. Evaluate each potential avenue for your work or skills with your personality in mind. Try a smattering of everything. Chances are you'll come up with two or three sales approaches that not only will consume all of your time, but also can make you feel comfortable in harness, which is, as Robert Frost said, what happiness is all about.

CHAPTER TWO

Designs on Success

If you weave a rug, it's a craft. If you nail the rug to a wall and call it a tapestry, it's fine art. The distinctions between arts and crafts are nebulous ones at best. Crafts are said to have utility, a function beyond aesthetic appreciation. Yet many decorative crafts exist for no other purpose than to bring pleasure to the eye. Crafts are said to be produced in quantity, as opposed to one-of-a-kind art objects. Yet artists produce numerous prints through lithography and photo art, and there are many craftspeople who never make a single copy of their original designs.

Yet there is one distinction between arts and crafts that seems to make sense. Crafts are created to serve the needs of other people. Arts are supposedly expressions of inner sensitivities and are thus self-serving. One reaches out, the other looks within. A fine distinction, perhaps, but one which makes a world of difference in how we go about creating our works. The craftsperson must be introspective in creating his or her original design, yet he or she cannot create without a great deal of consideration of the needs of the ultimate buyers. In other words, the craftsperson must, at times, set his or her ego aside, and take a sensitive look at the tastes of others.

Art and commerce must, by necessity, be interwoven by

the craftsperson. Design for its own sake will not succeed unless it also coincides with what the public wants and is willing to pay for. Conversely, a totally practical item with no design originality will have to compete with the mass-production world of pyrex and plastics and is inevitably doomed to failure. The successful craft is one that fits into the overall market, yet is distinctive enough to influence buyers, leading them in new directions. The crafts artist is no less creative because of the restrictions of marketability. In fact, the need to be aware of the overwhelming array of competitive items broadens understanding. Knowing what is commonplace is the first step to avoiding "cliche" crafts. And knowing one's customers produces a genuine respect for the variety of tastes and attitudes. An awareness develops that no matter how unique your design inclinations may be, there is a segment of the market with which you can communicate.

Creating for the craftsperson should begin, not in the studio, but in the streets and shops. Explore specialty shops, department stores, gift shops, and arts centers of all kinds. Read the ad sections of your newspaper. Subscribe to professional journals, such as *Craft Horizons* or *The Working Craftsman*. Scan the popular magazines, paying particular attention to the room displays in high-fashion publications. In Chapter Eleven we list numerous sources of information. Use every source you can to explore the crafts market you've chosen to investigate.

And don't restrict your inquiries just to the one area you've worked in up until now. Crafts are becoming more and more interdisciplinary. Fibers can be combined with metal work, painting, or leather to create fascinating new textures with more dimensions. Pottery can be combined with photography, or even silk screen, for new effects. A macrame craftsperson can learn pottery to create an integrated design for hanging plants.

Knowing what others are doing with success is a vital starting point. Being aware of the failures is one as well. A leather worker, for example, found far too much competition in making belts and purses. So he looked about and found a tremendous new market in leather-bound coffee mugs and place mats. In assisting native American ethnic groups develop profitable crafts, government sponsors have become expert at seeing how an Indian's grain-thrashing basket can be slightly redesigned into a bread basket or how an Appalachian wood chain whittler's skill can be reapplied to equally intricate wood puzzles and games.

You can, of course, simply lift a design from another part of the country or another field. Many do with varying degrees of success. But you can also improve on the original design in the process, creating something that is uniquely yours, yet also a proven winner. Modifying an existing design is especially easy to do when looking at popular manufactured items. Mass-produced designs have to be good or they won't sell, yet because of the machine limitations, they too often have to be underdesigned. Exaggerating or cleaning up the popular design is an excellent way of producing a sales winner.

The simplest way to check out the competition is to pose as a shopper. That may sound slightly dishonest, but you'll find that every commercial operation does it. Asking for a catalog of products because you might want to purchase them brings a far more immediate response than to introduce yourself as a fellow producer who wants the information in order to outdo them. Macy's doesn't tell Gimbels, but Macy's buyers do comparison shop at Gimbels every week.

If you are considering a traditional design, then it is imperative that you check out the competition to learn the parameters of the design's integrity. When making an early American vase, you don't want it to look Greek to knowledge-able buyers. "Design integrity" means that the product is correct for its tradition or time and that it is made from appropriate materials. Purists believe it should be made with the hand tools of the period as well, but this is far from neces-sary when mass sales are the ultimate aim. A lathe-turned pep-per mill of Amish design is just as appealing to the majority of buyers as a hand-carved one, and it's likely to be a lot more competitively priced. Should you choose to make true copies of originals, artifacts instead of facsimiles, then consider the tools along with all of the other historical or ethnic characteristics.

The distinction between a current design and one that is merely faddish is difficult to make. Americans are faddists, and no sooner does a design catch on than it is over. There are two ways craftspeople typically view the fad items. Some take advantage of fads for quick profits. The craftsperson can quickly produce a new design to get in on the peak of a fad, whereas a large-scale manufacturer is hampered by necessary time for retooling and scheduling. The craftsperson who keeps a small inventory of the transitory fashion items can thus profit. Many other craftspeople, however, feel that fads are too dangerous to jump into. A handcraft item, especially an expensive one, can remain on display for weeks, or even months, before it is sold. That's long enough for the fad to fizzle. Also, connecting your name and reputation with the unimaginative imitators and fad followers won't do your image much good. The decision is yours.

Studying the total market with all of its competitors is a lot like an astronaut learning astronomy. You can understand the universal qualities and the infinite range of possible directions, but you will get nowhere until you take the big step and decide on the particular cluster of stars you're shooting for. You have to narrow your target. No crafts appeal equally to the entire population. The successful craftsperson is one who learns early which group of buyers is drawn to his or her work, then aims designs specifically at pleasing that group. No product, or person, for that matter, appeals equally well to all people. Husbands and wives, fathers and sons, best friends—all disagree on what they like. Successful marketing is the knack of finding out which of those people tend to like what you have to offer, then going directly to them for a sale. It saves time and inspires success.

A customer profile is an essential if you are to find your own set of groupees. Who will most likely buy your design? How old are these customers? What interests and economic restrictions do they live with? What do their homes look like? How do they dress? The more you can find out about your potential customer, the easier it will be to serve those specific needs. Your work can thereafter reflect their needs and desires.

If you've already been selling your crafts for a time, then the customer profile is easy enough to make. Think about the people who have purchased your work up to now. Ask yourself if there are any common elements among them. If your work is displayed in a shop or gallery, hang around and watch the customers or interview the sales clerks on what kind of person has been buying your work. This process will give you not only direction, but also a great deal of insight into your own emotional and artistic makeup. For it's only a natural question to ask yourself next: Why does my work always seem to appeal to little old ladies or to the young and avant-garde?

A common error is to assume that your customers will naturally be exactly like you. That's just not the case. What you produce is influenced by your hands and who you are, but it has an identity all its own. Your customers may be like you; they may also be complete opposites. Making assumptions about them without doing a customer profile is a tactical error.

The federal government has done numerous studies of crafts buyers, and although they cannot tell you much about your specific following, they do give some insight into categories of crafts buyers. As they see it, there are essentially four common audiences: collectors, discriminating buyers, indigenous population, and tourists.

Collectors are the smallest group of buyers, yet the most prestigious. These individuals or representatives of institutions patronize galleries and fairs to find artistic items or those that are the finest examples of a craft tradition or regional form. Collectors are willing to pay more for such crafts, for they believe the pieces they choose will appreciate in value in their possession. Many look on collecting as an investment.

Discriminating buyers are looking for the unique and are willing to pay for it. They are the affluent suburbanites with high incomes who shop at all the better shops and boutiques to find items that reflect their personal tastes. The crafts market, because it is distinctive, is important to this group of buyers.

Indigenous population is the government's pretentious way of saying "neighborhood people." These are the customers with a sense of community; they like to identify the craft with the person who produced it. These same people will buy from a catalog or distant curio shop if they can identify with the designer or artist.

Tourists are the largest group of buyers for small crafts items. On holiday, they enjoy bringing back a purchase that is not only useful but also a subtle reminder of the trip itself. Highway gift shops, airport and hotel stores, theme parks, and regional fairs all attract large numbers of tourists.

Obviously, each of these four categories can, and should, be broken down into more specific audiences. Photo print collectors, for instance, tend to be young married people with limited incomes, while people who collect rare painted china pieces tend to be at or near retirement age and far more affluent. All collectors are far from alike. But the general categories do give you some idea of the markets and how you should approach them. You may find that you've been selling right along in one of these categories, yet haven't explored the others thoroughly. Do so, but remember that each of these broad groups has different motivations for buying. You may find that your work will sell to tourists because of regional appeal and to discriminating buyers because of the unique design and quality workmanship. With a little more analysis of the other markets, you could expand to sell to them all, remembering that you will have not one customer profile but four to consider.

Learn as much as you can about your customers: what magazines they read, what shows they attend, what their social and religious affiliations are. You might even find out what sports they follow. Buying the magazines your target customers buy and reading them for flavor and graphic style will tell you quite a bit about what items you can expect them to want in their homes. Armed with this knowledge, you can turn on your original designs for adaptations. Do your potential buyers lean to the modern or traditional, simplistic or ornate, inspirational or whimsical? Is there some other use that you can fit your original design to that would better fit your customers? Do the colors you choose complement or clash with those found in your customers' favorite magazines? Is the item you have in mind commonly offered in the magazine ads or in some other way provided to your customers, and if so, how can you make yours a bit different and more appealing?

In case you haven't guessed by now, the design is all-important if your crafts are to gain sales and your skills are to receive recognition. No matter how good a craftsperson you are, your ultimate success will depend on your design's sensitivity to your customers' tastes. It is so important, in fact, that we would suggest you go to any lengths to get good ones. If you can't seem to adapt a popular design to your needs or modify your design to popular tastes, then it would be worthwhile to pay a more experienced design person to help you out in this critical area. Find a successful craftsperson with selling designs and commission him or her to redesign your product. Give the professional designer a comprehensive customer profile and some idea of your objectives, and you can come out with a respectable product. For most in crafts, however, consulting a pro isn't necessary; craftspeople are normally attracted to their arts because of a desire to create new forms. But there is no shame in calling for him when you are staggering under a mental block.

Quality is significant in your final product, but not nearly so vital as the design itself. A customer rarely notices quality unless it is outstandingly bad. Crude cuts and stitches, rough edges, and visible glue will damage sales, but distinct quality, such as hand-rubbed wood or archival-mounted prints, will go unnoticed. The average buyer simply does not have the knowledge of your skill to know that you've taken those extra little pains to reach perfection.

Materials often fall under the category of general quality, and most customers do not notice them. But you can make the materials a strong selling point in themselves. A carpenter in Seattle uses the stumps of redwood trees to make coffee tables, night stands, and other distinctive items that emphasize the Northwestern origins. Crafts guilds in West Virginia have taken to making jewelry and other crafts items out of coal. Coal mining is a major part of the regional economy, and the vast majority of local people and tourists alike see coal as the distinctive aspect of this Appalachian area. Silver and coal cuff links and tie clasps are sold by the thousands of sets, not only in West Virginia, but in a six-state area. Find a material which characterizes your part of the country's terrain, industry, or historical traditions, and you have a built-in market for your crafts.

The most beautiful sound in the English language is that of your own name. You can sell people this self-recognition by including monograms or provisions for family crests and other personalizations. Because the craftsperson works in smaller quantities, this extra touch is possible. And if people are interested in themselves, they are also interested in you. Every crafts item has the story of its maker behind it. That can be incorporated into the label to provide added customer interest (we'll have more on labels later). Bringing sales down to a you-and-me level gives the normally indifferent world of marketing a warmth that most people like.

You can sell your crafts by emphasizing the materials,

workmanship, or personal interest, but each of these factors alone creates sales limits. Coal jewelry loses appeal in Alaska, and your personal story may not be as interesting on the opposite side of the country as it is to people in your own community. In the last analysis, all of these aspects simply serve to enhance the basic design. Develop a design that is uniquely your own yet fulfills the functional wants and desires of your customers, and you've taken the greatest leap possible into success at crafts.

CHAPTER THREE

Pricing for Profits

A well-designed crafts work must also be priced properly in order to be salable. If the price is too high, the piece won't be any more marketable than if the design is too extreme. But with a price that's too low, you won't make any profit, and that, remember, is your goal.

It's not hard to find a price which will be acceptable to both you and the buyer, but you'll have to do a little research and pencil work first.

Before you even begin to consider price, however, you have to answer an important question. Are you ready to produce your work in volume? You may have been happy weaving a few tablecloths and wall hangings for friends and relatives. Maybe you've even made enough pillows to display in your local guild shop. But are you ready to reproduce your design for dozens of place mats, or do you have the discipline to produce hundreds of pillows? Do you have the equipment and space?

One way to find out is to do it. Choose a favorite design and reproduce it as many times as you can before you go crazy. Try another item for about a week. At the end of the week ask yourself if you felt comfortable doing the work, because once the orders start coming in, you'll have to repeat your designs to fill them.

If your answer is "no," you have already determined part of your pricing structure. You won't be able to make the popularly priced items for wholesale distribution to shops. You might still make enough middle-priced pieces to sell at art fairs. Or if you could tolerate making only a few of each design, you'll want to restrict yourself to custom orders. Now you are talking about a different, higher price range.

It's important to confront the question of numbers so you don't find yourself caught with many unfilled orders and unhappy agents. There's room for all kinds of craftspeople. You just have to find the niche that suits your temperament and lifestyle.

A harder part of setting prices is trying to figure out what your value-conscious customers will be willing to pay for your work. This is difficult to gauge because it's subjective, based as much on a person's desire to own original and beautiful objects as on how much disposable income he has left after paying the mortgage. Some people with a lot of money to spare never learn to appreciate crafts, while others with very little cash love to be surrounded by works of art.

But nobody likes to pay more than he has to, so your first job is to find out what the competition is charging. Do a little research. If the potter in the next booth at the art fair is selling vases similar to yours at half the price you're asking, he'll get the sales, though your pots may be better made. At the end of the day, you'll be packing your unsold work to take home, the penalty for not doing your pricing homework.

Make a survey of products like yours to see what they are selling for. Go to art fairs, galleries, museum gift shops, and boutiques that carry crafts. Compare the type of item you make. Note the size, the number of pieces made of the same design (they're cheaper to make than one-of-a-kind pieces), and the quality as well as the price.

Don't forget your commercial competitors when making comparisons. Your leather belts or handmade mugs, for example, are also competing with those made by manufacturing companies. Find out what the department stores are charging. Some craftspeople I know who ignored this point were unaware that they were selling handmade pieces for less than the mass-merchandisers were getting. And even the least sophisticated buyer expects to pay more for crafts.

Still, your pieces have to be competitively priced if they are to sell. Of course, some craftspeople have developed fine reputations and can demand higher prices for their work. A dress by Christian Dior also costs a lot more than one made by an unknown designer, and there are always some people willing to pay for the status of wearing the original.

Crafts have only recently begun to command the high prices fine arts always have. One well-established glass blower goes to a midwestern art fair each year just to sell to three or four local collectors who know his work and are willing to pay $150 to $1,100 for his pieces. Even a few sales make his trip worthwhile. Perhaps you'll reach that level too, but for now you have to keep your eye on what the market will bear.

You can justify some higher prices if the materials used cost more. A ring made of gold will obviously be more expensive than a silver ring because, as everyone knows, gold costs more than silver. A customer also may be willing to pay extra for a necklace made of unusual, imported beads than for one made of ordinary materials. The key is that the buyer has to be able to appreciate the difference. It's unlikely most people will understand enough about your work, say, in creating an elaborate glaze for a piece of pottery when they can buy similar pots across the street at lower prices, even if the glaze is less beautiful.

Consider other psychological factors also. If your price is too low, a potential buyer becomes suspicious that something is wrong with the piece. You can lose sales when prices are too much below the going rate as well as when they're too high.

Keep in mind that before a prospective buyer asks the price of your work, he has already made a tentative decision to buy it. He probably thinks, "That wooden piece would be perfect on my coffee table," before he adds, "if it's not too expensive." He knows the balance in his checking account. He can't consider a Cadillac when a Chevrolet is all he can afford. Within reason, though, we've all bought things that may have cost more than we wanted to spend.

It is important to stay within the price range you determine for your work. "I don't display inexpensive pieces with my expensive work," an established craftsman told me, "because it cheapens my costlier items." The reverse is also true. A customer attracted to your work is comfortable with the price and is not likely to pay a lot more for one of your pieces priced significantly higher.

There is one way you can show your virtuosity on a few one-of-a-kind pieces, even though you may be aiming for a moderately-priced market. Use them for display. Weavers, for instance, often make a few huge wall hangings for use as backdrops at art fairs. Their attractive booths draw customers, who then buy the less expensive pieces. But concentrate your efforts on items within the price range you've established.

When you have settled on the pace of work you can do and

have determined the price others charge for similar objects, you're ready to figure out whether your work can be produced profitably. This is the easy part of pricing because it's objective: you calculate the costs of your production. If you can make the piece within salable range and realize a profit, you're in business.

Some craftspeople work the opposite way by calculating their own costs first and then setting the selling price. It's more realistic to work from the top down. Then, if you find you can't produce the piece for a competitive price, you can try to make the necessary adjustments in production or drop the whole item and look for another one you can make profitably. Remember, this book is about selling crafts, not giving them away.

"I never calculate the cost of my labor because no one would be able to afford my pieces if I did," one beginning sculptor told me. She'd better enjoy what she's doing, because she isn't making a cent of profit. You have to charge for your labor as well as for your materials, overhead, selling expenses, and profit allowance. These elements make up the wholesale price of your craft.

The time you invest at the beginning to itemize your costs will be rewarded by greater profits in the end. It's not hard to do, but it does take some accurate bookkeeping. The only tools you need are a sharp pencil and a ledger, or costs book (available at stationery stores).

The most obvious item you have to consider in the production costs are the materials you use. Even the most economically naive craftsperson is concerned about recovering out-of-pocket expenses for buying materials. By keeping close records, you'll be sure to regain all your outlay.

Those who use reclaimed materials, such as old metal cans

for tin sculptures or driftwood, also have a way to charge for materials. Since these require time to collect, time which is taken away from your production, you are justified in making up the loss. Record how long the collection takes you, and give yourself a reasonable wage per hour.

It's important to include every single thing you use to produce your work. Although you most likely will not forget the major materials, keep track of small items like thread or glue, too. These can add up to important expenses when you work in volume.

You should try to arrive at a material cost per item produced. Because this is often difficult to calculate, it may be more practical to figure the cost per dozen or hundred, depending on what you make and how long it takes. One method is to record the amount of material used each day, week, or even month, and divide it by the number of items produced during that time.

For example, a craftsman who makes sculptures out of corrugated cardboard (I actually met one who did!) bases his figures on a week's work. He knows he can make about ten sculptures from one design each day, so he calculates his costs per fifty, a typical week's work. His weekly entry for materials' costs might look like this:

CARDBOARD	50 pieces use 1 yd. each 50 yds. @ $1/ yd.	$50.00
GLUE	1 qt. each week	5.00
VARNISH	5 gals. to fill vat for dipping sculptures @ $4/ gal.	20.00
MIRRORS	to decorate sculptures 50 @ $.50	25.00
	TOTAL COST	$100.00

Number of items: 50

COST PER ITEM: $2.00 each

Try to find out if there is going to be a price increase on your next order for materials before you begin to figure the costs. Although future changes are probably inevitable, you don't want to have to raise your prices as soon as you set them. It also makes sense to shop around before settling on a certain supplier so you can take advantage of the best offer. Buying materials in bulk may also be economical, because suppliers often give small discounts for large orders. But don't do this until you are sure you will have enough orders to justify the outlay.

Some suppliers also will give you a small discount for prompt payment. Most bills are not due until the end of the month, but some allow you a 2 percent discount if you pay the bill within ten days. Any small reduction adds up when you think in terms of many orders over a long time.

Your itemization should also include shipping costs or other expenses incurred in getting the materials.

Labor costs are more difficult to calculate than materials, but they are just as important. Beginning craftspeople are wrong to ignore the price of their time in producing their work. Although it may seem far away, you have to anticipate the time when you may have to hire someone to help you with production. Their salary will have to be paid, so right from the start you need to figure labor costs.

Again, the goal is to calculate the amount per piece, but that is tricky. Although a jeweler may make a necklace from start to finish in one sitting, more often a crafts work is made in stages. Therefore the actual time spent on each piece is difficult to arrive at, but not impossible.

Try to find a convenient unit of measure. A potter may want to calculate costs based on each time he fires his kiln. If it holds one hundred pieces and has taken him a week to make the pieces—from preparing the clay, throwing the pots, glazing and decorating, to loading the kiln—then his labor costs can be figured per hundred pieces.

Be sure to keep track of the number of hours spent on each stage of production. Have a notebook handy with the stages clearly set out and note the exact number of minutes or hours of each stage. This is important for two reasons. First, using our potter as an example, he has to know how many hours were spent on the hundred pieces he fired that week in order to know how much his labor costs were. If he spent fifty hours making the hundred pieces, each piece took thirty minutes. Then all the potter has to do is arrive at a charge-per-hour for his labor. As a beginner, you may have to accept a lower rate for your labor than you feel you're worth because you're probably not as efficient as you will be. But don't allow yourself less than the minimum wage, because that's the least you would have to pay someone to replace your efforts.

Efficiency is the second reason to keep close track of how long each stage of production lasts. If your production costs are excessive, meaning you have to charge more for your piece than people will pay, you'll have to analyze your methods to see where you can streamline. Your records will show you where you are spending too much time.

Before calculating labor costs, it's a good idea to experiment for a week or two to see how long it takes you to make your product. Keep track of the first week's time and compare it to the second. If working with individual pieces, note the time it takes to make the first one and the last. Does your efficiency improve? It should, and you can then base your costs on your fastest time.

Your time records may help you decide whether to hire someone else to do the routine tasks so you can concentrate on the more creative parts of the production. One successful potter, for example, hires a student to mix the clay and clean up. He has to pay only the minimum wage, and he earns a lot more working at his wheel and decorating his pieces during the time saved from these other jobs.

It also requires effort to make the designs for your craft. Many people feel this is the most enjoyable part of being a craftsperson. They don't even think they can put a price on their creativity. You have to. You can figure design costs the same as labor, calculating it on a per-hour basis, or you can just decide what price each item ought to include for design.

This is another area where you can keep costs down in the early stages of your career. But do recognize your design efforts in some way. You may consider writing off the part of the design costs that you don't charge for as a business loss on your taxes. But consult your accountant on this point first.

Thinking about labor costs in a businesslike fashion will

force you to become more professional about your work. Too often craftspeople are accused of not being reliable businesspeople. Many don't pay their bills on time. Others sleep late, taking days off whenever they feel like it. Once you think of your labor in terms of dollars per hour, you will realize that each hour away from your bench means less money in your pocket. A successful weaver said, "I work every day, rain or shine, whether I feel like it or not." And his profits reflect his hard work.

Part of your attempt to become more efficient will have to focus on reducing the nonproductive time that is part of every craftsperson's life. You have to clean up, send out bills, order and pick up materials, talk to other craftspeople, read journals, and attend to many other details that you can't charge anyone for. Still, these tasks reduce your productivity. If you calculate your labor costs at $5 an hour and put in forty hours a week, you'll make $200—just for production. But if you have to spend an additional ten hours a week at nonchargeable tasks, your hourly rate goes down to $4 an hour ($200 divided by fifty hours).

To find out how you are spending your time, keep a diary for a week or two. Write down each quarter-hour during the day before you start, and fill in your activities as you go along. Include lunch, coffee breaks, telephone calls, and any interruptions which take you away from your work. You may be shocked to see how much nonproductive time you whittle away during the day.

Labor and materials comprise what is usually thought of as the direct production costs. Overhead is the third element to be considered. Whether you occupy a small corner of your basement or rent a studio, the expense of maintaining it establishes the overhead costs which have to be counted in the selling price. Overhead refers to the cost of rent, heat, electricity, water, telephone, insurance, taxes, and repairs.

It's easy to figure out these expenses if you rent a studio where you do all your work. You just have to keep all your bills. But chances are you do your craft in a room or part of a room in your home. What then? You have to calculate the percentage of your home used only for your work and take that percentage of the bills for the entire house. Many of your figures will be based on an educated guess as well as specific bills. Although a potter may know exactly how much electricity was used to fire his kiln because it has a meter, he can't know exactly how many kilowatts were used to light his workroom. These expenses are justifiable parts of calculating your selling costs, but you must be scrupulously honest.

Other costs which relate to your work include office supplies, postage, delivery and freight, packing materials, and cleaning expenses. Don't forget to consider the losses on crafts work that break or become unsalable for other reasons. These can be a major expense for people who sell on consignment. Stores will return shopworn pieces to you, and you'll have to absorb the loss.

Generally, the overhead should come to about 35 percent of the wholesale price.

You'll want to find the cost per piece, just as you did with material and labor costs. Perhaps a monthly unit of measure would be useful, divided by the number of pieces produced during that time.

The fourth element you need to calculate the wholesale cost of your work is one many beginners forget to include: the profit. This should be calculated separately from your labor costs. It's the return you get for the whole project—for the creativity that went into it, the skills required to carry it out, and the risks undertaken. In short, for being an entrepreneur instead of just a laborer.

A reasonable profit is about 10 percent of the wholesale price, but that is only an estimate. Many beginners have to reduce the profit because their overall costs make their work too expensive to sell. But always include some amount as profit, even if only a few cents.

The expense of selling your work is the last element in your calculations. Some people include it in overhead costs. To find markets for your crafts, you may spend time going to shops. Perhaps you sell directly to wholesale houses without the benefit of an agent. Or you might travel all over the country selling at art fairs. Whatever your method, each hour away from your studio means less production. You have to regain the loss by charging for your selling time. Also include your travel expenses, such as transportation, motel, and food. A wholesale agent would charge about 15 percent of the wholesale price to find your customers. That's a good figure to use when calculating your own selling expenses.

Another way to sell your own wares is through your own studio or shop. As the person who markets the piece as well as produces it, you are entitled to the same profit other retailers get. The retail price in a store is usually double the wholesale price (the price the store owner paid to get the product). The difference is called the mark-up. This mark-up covers the store owner's expenses and profit. Although you have already realized a profit in the wholesale price, you should also get this second profit if you sell to the public.

The wholesale price of your work, then, consists of:

MATERIALS + LABOR + OVERHEAD (INCLUDING SELLING COSTS) + PROFIT = WHOLESALE PRICE
WHOLESALE PRICE + MARK-UP (usually 100 percent) = RETAIL PRICE.

Thinking of these elements as percentages: labor and materials are usually about 40 percent of the wholesale price, overhead about 35 percent, selling costs about 15 percent, and profit on the wholesale price about 10 percent. And the retail price is generally double the wholesale price.

What do you do if, after calculating all your costs, you find the selling price is out of line with other products like yours? This is the hard part of pricing. The most likely answer is to cut costs. The first place to look is your productivity, or labor costs. Find ways to be more efficient so you can make more items in less time. Analyze your records to see how you are spending your time, and look for short cuts. Perhaps you're spending too much time creating one-of-a-kind objects that are too expensive. Modifying the design so the items take less time to produce may be in order. If you can make a ring in an hour and a half instead of two hours, your efficiency improves significantly. You can also reduce labor costs by reducing the hourly amount you're paying yourself. Even though you may feel you should get $10 an hour, you may have to accept $6 if your selling price isn't competitive.

Maybe you can cut the costs of materials without affecting the quality of the pieces. Make the belts narrower or the pillows smaller for the same price. Or check to see if another supplier sells the materials for less.

You may be able to make some reductions in the overhead costs and profit, too. But, in the end, your productivity is the key. The more you can produce per hour, the more money you'll make. And it doesn't have to affect the quality of your work.

One prolific and highly-regarded potter, Steve Jepson from Florida, said, "Making a lot of pottery makes my work better, not worse, because it makes me more efficient." In addition to his financial success (he makes more than the president of the university where he teaches), he has received several merit awards and has a piece in the Smithsonian. Who said that quantity corrupts quality?

It is possible that after making all the reductions you can think of, your piece will still cost more than others you compared it to in your market research. What then? Your productivity will probably improve as you gain more experience, but you can't delay the mortgage payments that long. The solution to the problem is drastic: you have to design a different piece.

Some artists feel they have to make certain "bread and butter" designs that sell well and earn them enough to finance their efforts on elaborate works that require more effort and may not be so profitable. Your market comparisons should have shown you what kinds of items in your craft were most popular. You may have to consider switching to one of them. As crafts become more and more popular, the competition increases. Crafts shoppers become more selective and price-conscious.

When you arrive at a salable price for your work, there are a number of ways to market it. You can sell at wholesale prices to retail stores, either yourself or through an agent, or you can sell it yourself, at retail prices, in your own shop, studio, art fair booth, or through direct mail orders.

If you're selling directly to the public, avoid bargain-basement mentality when pricing your wares. Don't, for example, mark an object $.99 instead of $1.00. This popular trick is completely inappropriate in the crafts world. Mark your pieces in even dollars. Also, don't charge less per item if a customer wants more than one. Craftspeople refer to this practice as "trading up." If your pottery mugs are $5 each, and you sell two for $9, you are trading up. The principle is that selling more volume will increase your profits, even at slightly lower prices. This may be true when working with high-volume items, but in your studio or art fair retail sales, the volume will not be great enough to justify the commercialism of the approach. It may turn off more customers than it will increase sales. Also, if you sell to the public, as well as to stores, charge the same price for your work that the retail stores do. It is poor business practice and unfair to both the stores and their customers to sell for less.

The only discount that may be justified is to your wholesale buyers. Trade discounts are common for bills that are paid quickly. You might offer your wholesale customers the standard 2 percent discount if they pay their bill within ten days instead of the normal thirty days. The advantage of this is getting the cash promptly so you can put it to work in other ways for your business.

Your investment in making your crafts will be profitable only if you can sell them. Good businesspeople watch their inventory carefully to see how quickly their stock "turns over." As the products sell and return cash to the business, the money can be reinvested to make more items. The faster the turnover, the greater the profit.

As a retailer you have to watch your stock, too. Be aware of those pieces which sell quickly and those which don't. A piece which doesn't sell is obviously not making you any profit. Consider dropping it from your inventory or redesigning it.

You must always ask yourself whether the time you spend in selling would be better used in production. Art fairs, for example, should be carefully scrutinized, because they can be a drain on your productivity. Say you make $150 in profit at a three-day fair. Could you have made more if you had stayed home and worked in your studio? Of course, many artists enjoy the direct contact with buyers and the camaraderie of other craftspeople they meet at these fairs. They don't want to give that up.

But once you enter the business of selling crafts, you have to be ruthless about your time. In the business world, time is money—especially when you are the only one generating what can be sold.

You can make your time count more by keeping accurate records of all your production costs: labor, materials, overhead, selling, and profit. Once you develop a habit of doing this, it won't take long, for you have to do it only once for each item you make. But precise recordkeeping is essential to profitable pricing.

CHAPTER FOUR

Selling on Consignment

In the best of all possible worlds, every merchant would buy crafts items outright and hand over hard cash upon delivery. But this isn't an ideal world for craftspeople. Competitors are many, outlets for crafts few. To clear a place for your crafts on a merchant's shelf, you must offer a real-world compromise to demanding cash. That compromise is most often selling on consignment.

To sell on consignment simply means that you leave your items in a shop, boutique, or gallery and don't get paid until your crafts are actually sold. That could be weeks, months, or never. In effect, you're underwriting the merchant, providing his stock and tying up your work. Crafts crusaders say this approach ought to be consigned to a wastebasket. Perhaps, but until a better method is devised that is acceptable to both the merchant and craftsperson, consignment is a fact of life.

In many cases, consignment is the only choice. If you are working with precious metals, throwing large elegant pots, or looming wall-sized weavings, the price tags may limit your market. Few merchants can afford to invest a great deal in one stock item. Or if you're new on the sellers' scene, with no track record to indicate probable sales, then consignment selling is the way to prove your work without forcing the small business proprietor to take a chance on you.

While the experts swear at consignment selling, many successful craftspeople swear by it. Once the initial waiting-for-sales period has passed, consignment cash flow can be as steady as outright sales, provided your merchandise is salable. And because your share of the sale price is higher with consignment than it would be if you sold wholesale, it can be even more profitable for you in the long run.

If you are an otherwise unknown handcrafter, the consignment arrangement provides needed exposure and the important first step toward outright selling. It is also a shot at trying to market new, untested products, of finding out whether there is a market for your string bags or hand-blown finger bowls. And it is a method of relieving a surplus that may be collecting dust in your workshop. Consignment is a kind of partnership agreement. You add to the shop's inventory, and they, in turn, advertise, pay insurance, salaries, and other overhead, and give you an on-going weatherproof display.

There are all kinds of shops. The important thing is to find the right one for your products. A recent study showed that in 85 percent of the situations in which craft items failed to sell, the products had been misplaced. The seller did not select his shop discriminately. Just as bulls in china shops don't work, you're gambling if you try to place swarthy leather belts in a setting with gold and silver filigree jewelry. The example may be extreme, but the message is simple: don't place your work just anywhere to get exposure. Take the time to find that right spot to get it sold.

You can begin your shop hunt in the yellow pages of your telephone directory. Starting close to home will enable you to visit a number of stores and give you a feel for what would be right for your products. The ability to judge comes with practice.

If you're in a marketer's void, public libraries carry directories for other cities. Books that are helpful include *Contemporary Crafts Market Place* and *Craft Shops-Galleries USA* (American Crafts Council, 44 West 53rd St., New York, NY 10019), *American Crafts Guide* (edited by Marian May, Gousha Publications, San Jose, CA), and the *Hotel Redbook,* which lists gift shops located in hotels throughout the country. These sources include state-by-state listings, selling policies, telephone numbers, and the name of a contact person in the shop.

The easiest shops to approach are the nonprofit shops. Housed in Y's, churches, or civic clubs, these mini-business ventures seek out local craftspeople and promote their work. They provide exposure for the handcrafter and a small income for the organization. Such shops are generally run by volunteers. Consignment arrangements are the rule, with the shop getting 20 to 25 percent of the selling price. Your products will have to be judged acceptable by the shop manager, but this is usually handled by an informal interview.

Step up to boutiques, gift shops, and stores that handle only craft items if you're ready for a slightly more competitive market. Such shops are typically found in tourist areas, high-traffic shopping centers, and college towns. They deserve your in-person visit and approval.

Successful craftswoman Judy Myers says that when she is searching for a new outlet, she always makes personal visits. "I can usually tell if my work is going to sell once I've visited a store," Judy says. "I just have a good feeling about it when it's right."

It may take a little practice before you can make such an

immediate evaluation. One way to begin your assessment is to pretend you're a shopper. Look around. Is the shop inviting? Is the help friendly? What kinds of things do they handle? How are the prices? Is the clientele Fifth Avenue or bluejeans? Which type will buy your craft?

When things look pretty good, switch hats and play seller. In this role you'll need to determine if there is a niche for your work. You won't want to place your handcrafted items in a store selling factory-produced ones of the same kind, because the factory-produced ones will probably be cheaper than yours. What about display space? If your jewelry needs glass cases, and the shop uses rough wood shelving, tell your sculpting friends about it, but take your work elsewhere. Or if your weavings would look great against a brick wall, and their walls are mirrors, walk right out.

When you've finally connected, the setting is great, and the vibrations are right (and it won't take long), you are ready to approach the manager.

Stop in some weekday afternoon and tell the owner how much you like the shop. If you can mention that Zanzibar Tanhide, the best-known leather crafter in town, recommended that you approach this particular shop, so much the better.

After the owner's appreciative response, you can ask for an appointment to bring in the specific items that you think would "complement her stock." If business is slow, she might be interested in seeing what you have right then. Be prepared. Have several samples of your work in your car or a half dozen slides or pictures in your pocket.

Once you've made a successful contact, prepare for your first appointment. Know what you're going to say about your product.

After show-and-tell you'll want to talk business. Find out when and how often you can bring in your goods. There are many other questions to be answered to your satisfaction before you leave your goods with the store. The best way to handle this—or any business transaction—is to put your understandings in writing.

Some craftspeople consign only to shops where they know the owners personally and maintain friendly, verbal agreements. One California glass blower I spoke to says, "I see this as a matter of trust. We have a partnership. I fill up his shelves, and he pays me my percentage at the end of each month. It's getting by with a little help from my friends."

That's nice, but chances are you'll want to do better than "get by." What if his friends go deeply into debt, sell out, die, or enlarge to the point where the facility is managed by someone else? Without a written agreement he could lose out.

A consignment agreement is a contract. It provides clear information about what is expected of both parties and can be upheld in small claims court, if necessary. A shopkeeper will take your relationship a lot more seriously if you know what you want and put it in writing. And there's no reason why you still can't be friends.

Designing the contract is up to you. It doesn't have to be complicated to cover all significant points. Start with what it's all about: money. When a shop sells a consigned article, it keeps a specified percentage of the sale, ranging from 10 to 40 percent, with 33 percent being the most common figure. This means that the retailer collects about one third of the marked price as a service charge for handling your item. But the exact percentage is negotiable. If you are providing one-of-a-kind items and selling them exclusively to one shop, aim for the high figure. If you're selling through a YMCA or church group, you can expect to be dealing on the low end of the scale.

When will you get paid? There are choices. Thirty days from the date of your invoice is one option, or, if you deliver work on an irregular basis, the first or fifteenth of each month might be more suitable.

The duration of the agreement should also be part of the contract. It could be anywhere from 30 to 60 days in small shops to 6 months to a year in the more prestigious galleries. Check with other craftspeople who deal with the establishment, or ask the shopowner if he has a standard period for handling consignments.

On the contract termination date most shops return unsold articles to the craftsman, but you needn't take your goods and go home. The shopkeeper may be willing to buy your unsold merchandise at wholesale prices or to renew the consignment agreement. You can include these options in your contract.

What about damage? Any items damaged in the shop or enroute being returned to you should be the responsibility of the shop. You should not accept returned merchandise in an unsalable condition. A statement saying, "Items not returned to the craftsperson in original and perfect condition and items not returned at all will remain the property of_____shop or gallery and the craftsperson shall be paid his full percentage of 66 percent at the expiration of the agreement," will protect you against damage or theft.

It is best to consign to shops close to home, not only because you can maintain a personal contact with the store, but also because there will be no need to ship your goods. If shipping is necessary, agree to share the cost equally with your outlet.

Protect yourself against any eventuality. What if the

business goes bankrupt with a lot of your work in stock? Unless you specify otherwise, your $500 tapestry could go to the shop's creditors. A brief statement that says in case of bankruptcy all consigned merchandise reverts to the craftsman and cannot be transferred, will cover you.

The agreement should reflect the shop owner's concerns, too. For instance, he should not be responsible for unsold items left more than ten days (or any specified length of time) after contract termination, and you may wish to give the shop exclusive right to market some of your items.

Finally, your signature and the consignor's will seal the deal. Date the contract and provide your buyer with a copy and an invoice for all your merchandise.

If pushing your pencil through all of this is a bit much, you can order fifty consignment forms for $2.50 from the Guild of American Craftsmen (Box 645, Rockville, MD 20851) that will cover the basics for protecting your work. Also, *Career Opportunities in Crafts* by Elyse Sommer (Crown Publishers, 1977), contains a comprehensive agreement that you might want to modify to suit your own situation.

After you have reached agreement with the store owner and have left your goods, stop back periodically to check out the display of your works, hear any customer feedback, and discuss future arrangements. Here, again, it's a great advantage if the shop is nearby.

Keep in mind that consigning is a first step. Many stores buy crafts items in a variety of ways. They often combine consignment with direct wholesale buying. If your products sell well, the shop owner should eventually be willing to buy from you directly. Don't wait for him to suggest it, or you may forever be a consignee. It's to his advantage to take work on consignment, because there's little risk for him. But it's to your advantage to sell outright. You have your money right away, and shopkeepers are less apt to push your consigned merchandise than that which they have money invested in. After you prove to the merchant that your craft is making money, you have a strong argument to have him purchase it outright. At that point you can make the glorious transition from consigning to direct sales.

Soon you may be ready for a greater challenge: the department store market. The larger, more expensive stores are the best choice for handcrafted items because they serve a clientele that will pay for unique and well-done work. There is usually a buyer for each department in a large store. Find out which one might handle your products and make an appointment to see him or her.

There are two things to keep in mind when dealing with the department store buyer. First, if your product is small, he or she may want to purchase it in quantity. Therefore, have a good supply on hand before you promise to fill a contract. Second, because you are competing with factory-produced goods, your work must be unique if you plan to cash in.

Uniqueness goes beyond design. A strong selling point is to promise to produce your craft exclusively for that particular store. You've scored a point if you can guarantee that no one within a one-hundred-mile radius of their parking lot is selling this same item. If you care to go for two, offer to do a little promoting of your own. A craft that can be demonstrated is always a drawing card from a buyer's point of view (more on wholesaling in Chapter Six).

The world of vending your wares is not limited to shops and stores. Galleries and museums are also outlets for craftsworks. If you wish to try gallery marketing, however, you must appraise your work very carefully. And on a scale of one-to-ten you had better be in the eight-and-up quality range. Fine art is the mainstay of these operations, and the easily duplicated pot or the tapestry of "in" design will not find a buyer in a gallery.

A gallery or museum caters to clients. Gallery patrons are not window-shopping. They are art admirers and art purchasers. They attend showings and receptions. If until now you've dealt mainly with shops and fairs, educate yourself about galleries before plunging in.

The temptations to plunge in are many. The attentive audience is your first bonus. Next, most gallery items sport high price tags. Gallery openings and showings are often newsworthy events, and you're likely to find your name in print, in local as well as regional and state publications. And finally, once you've established your niche in a gallery, the gallery's clientele becomes your clientele.

At the gallery stage the commitment to your work goes beyond salable colors or patterns. It is no longer the hobby craft it once might have been. It is now a true artistic expression. People viewing your work will be enriched by it. Those purchasing it see more than just a handcrafted, unusual gold ring or a forceful wood sculpture. They are selecting an objet d'art. Be honest with yourself. Not everyone is cut out for gallery showings. In fact, not everyone wants to be in this class of artisans. In assessing your work, consult articles published in *Craft Horizons, Art in America,* or *Art News.* There will be guidelines and suggestions. Just keep in mind that this is a tough nut to pot, hang, carve, quilt, or hook.

Galleries are easy to find. They are listed in the same sources that cover retail shops. There are fewer of them, so selection is seldom a prerogative. When you find one nearby, consider yourself blessed. Most galleries are located in the larger metropolitan areas, so you may be forced to make frequent pilgrimages to the city if you live in a rural community. But if you receive gallery recognition, the trips will be worthwhile. Not all galleries accept crafts-related items, so you'll save yourself discouragement if you invest a few dimes to trace this information before you visit.

Unlike the casual approach to the retail shop, interviewing in a gallery is more formal. Send a letter that includes your background, awards, exhibition experience, affiliations with artisan's organizations, and recommendations by outstanding craftspeople in your field. And, because galleries are in business to sell art, if you can offer a list of names and addresses of clients or customers who could be invited to a showing, this bit of information might be what it takes to convince them to take a chance with your craft. State that you will telephone on a specific day to arrange an appointment to show samples and slides of your work.

You may be turned down flatly. This is not necessarily a reflection on you or your work. Galleries often carry year-long consignments with artists and simply may not have room to add your work. Or your particular craft may be new or too experimental for them.

If you do get an opportunity to present your work, do not make the mistake of hauling in boxes of samples. This will immediately label you an amateur, and one experience with this technique will teach you not to repeat it. The rare exceptions might be in silver or goldsmithing where the items are small and manageable. The gallery will have a slide projector for your showing. They may even wish to keep the slides for a short period for further review. Nothing but professional-quality slides will do.

When you have made an impression on a gallery and they are ready to talk business, it is time to, once again, ask questions, discuss, resolve problems, and put your agreements in writing. Because most galleries work exclusively with consignment sales, they will not be surprised when you insist on covering all of the details.

Unlike retail shops, which keep 10 to 40 percent of the retail price for handling your work, galleries usually charge 50 to 66 percent. In addition, you might be asked to share in the expenses of a reception-exhibition or a catalog of gallery items. If this is the case in your gallery, insist on nothing above the 50 percent figure. Keep in mind that your fine work may be tied up for as long as a year and that in sharing expenses you are also supporting and selling works of other artists.

The same potential problems present with consignment selling to shops, boutiques, and other retail outlets are present with galleries. The need for clear communication, and the use of invoices, receipts, and written agreements cannot be stressed enough. Attention to the detail side of consignment will go a long way to enhance your expertise in marketing your craft.

A step above galleries are museums, the top rung of the craftsperson's success ladder. Being selected to exhibit in a museum is not only prestigious, but, eventually, very profitable.

A midwestern potter told me that the market in museum sales is very limited, but when he does make a sale to a museum shop (direct, not consigned), it can buy his clay for a whole year. Unfortunately there aren't enough museums to go around.

Well-known museums, such as the Baltimore Museum of

Art, Detroit Institute of Arts, the Museum of Atlanta, and the Smithsonian, are a few that have recognized the art value of crafts works. The same directories that list crafts retail shops also include museums.

If you can sell or consign to a museum shop, by all means do so. The general guidelines for shops and galleries apply to museums, and even if a poorer percentage must be realized, the prestige and credentials of dealing with a museum are incentive enough to try for this, the top spot.

Whether your work is consigned to boutiques or sold directly to museums, there is one final consideration that you can profit by—the calendar. Remember that retailers must plan and stock their inventory from three to nine months in advance. Take a minute to flip through a calendar that notes all significant holidays and then subtract three to six months. You'll have a good idea of when to approach buyers. You probably have a better chance of unloading your more expensive and seasonal wares in June if you're aiming for the December holidays than you might in November when the customers are thinking about gift buying. November is the time to show your stuffed bunnies and spring creations.

The smaller the shop the more apt you are to be able to crowd the calendar when it comes to seasonal sales. The department store, however, will not even consider a Christmas item after Labor Day. And because December is a time for major retailing, you might try for a large inventory in June.

The outlets are many, but the methods are few. Consigning is the way to work into direct selling, whether it is to the non-profit shop, hospital gift shop, or nationally-known gallery. The kicker is the research and preparation. But the effort is worth it if you really want to get your foot in the door.

CHAPTER FIVE

Everybody Loves a Fair

No one knows how the first arts and crafts show began, but one can imagine a few Neanderthal women gleaming over neighboring cave dwellers' tiger-tooth trinkets and dragging their mates along for a fair exchange of menacing grunts and threatening gestures.

Today's shows are far more sophisticated, friendlier, and offer a wider variety of products then those of our predecessors. They also offer you one of the most affable ways of selling your wares. Unlike yesterday's craftspeople, who traveled by foot or animal-drawn wagon through uncharted trails, present-day artisans clip along highways by van, camper, bus, car, and trailer from one city to another or, in many cases, to nearby states.

Depending upon how you work it, making the show circuit can mean being away from home and studio only a few hours or as much as several weeks or even months at a stretch. Therefore, the type of products you sell, family responsibilities, personal and professional obligations, where you live, and your personality are important factors to be weighed before throwing the dog into the car and heading toward the rising sun with your wares.

A large number of shows take place at any one time, and

familiarizing yourself with the variety, how they function, and the pros and cons will help in making the right decision about the best show for you.

Finding out about shows is easy. Word of mouth, newspapers, newsletters from craft organizations, magazines such as *Artisan Crafts, Craft Horizon,* and *Outlook;* quarterly show calendars, the US Department of Commerce, the Chamber of Commerce, and art museums will provide you with a full schedule. Also, you can visit arts and crafts schools, art institutes, and college campuses where notices of pending craft-related events are often displayed. Contacting the American Crafts Council (44 West 53rd Street, New York, NY 10019, 212-977-8989) will further add to your show itinerary.

After scanning the piles of pamphlets, you will see that some shows are amateur events and others are professional. Both types are held in shopping malls, rented space at state or county fair grounds, school gyms, churchyards, community buildings, along street curbs, flea markets, and so on. Non-profit groups raising money for charitable causes find arts and crafts shows a natural. Local talent is plentiful and space offered by a church, club, or school is adequate, free or inexpensive, and conveniently located. A volunteer working with a small group organizes and runs the festival. These social gatherings may not be so well organized as one that is professionally handled, but the enthusiasm and hard work of the amateur director usually compensates for any shortcomings. If you have never sold at fairs, this is a good way of getting acquainted with the ins and outs.

Professional shows are handled by full-time promoters who make their livings this way. They have their own sets of rules and charge either an entry fee ranging between $10 for small shows to $100 and up for prestigious ones, or a 10 to 30 percent commission on gross sales. At some fairs you will be required to pay a combination of both fees.

A portion of the money covers your allotted space, which normally measures ten feet by ten feet. Areas are usually arbitrarily assigned, but you may have a choice as promoters become familiar with you and your work. If there is a choice, be sure to get your request in early because the location of the booth can mean the difference between a prosperous show or a poor one. You'll want space near the heavily traveled paths or by food concession stands.

Some of the fee should also go toward publicity and advertising. You're there to sell, and if the public knows nothing about the exhibition, attendance will be lacking and sales scant.

In addition to apprising the public of the show, the promoter's responsibility is to make sure you know well in advance the opening date, where it's going to be held, the starting and ending dates, any special arrangements made with lodging establishments, and a listing of conveniently located restaurants, camp grounds, and other services.

It's hard work organizing and running a show. A polished director will shine. Some show organizers, however, appear to have matters in hand, when, in fact, important details slip through their fingers. Shy away from these people. You will end up paying more than the entrance fee in grief and disappointment.

Choosing a *good* show is difficult. Even seasoned artisans make mistakes, but there are several points to check out. First, talk to others who have attended the show before. Get some feedback on how they did, their complaints, and if they would do the same show again. Was there an abundance of one type of craftsperson? Think of the horrors of having your weavings walled in by the weavings of three others. Find out how long the show's been in existence and who is running it. Check the overall attendance, how many craftspeople exhibited, and what the gross sales were. Also, the material sent to participants by the organizer can often be a good indication of the show's pending success. Is it detailed and well organized or haphazardly put together?

Shows can be "open" or "juried." An open show lets in anyone with something to sell, provided there's sufficient room and the fee is paid. With little or no guidelines to follow, quality and shoddy products can be displayed side by side. In fact, many of the items may not be crafts at all, but rather a collection of odds and ends one finds at a garage sale, cheap imported goods, or items made from kits. This is not a true arts and crafts show and can be particularly frustrating to the talented artisan who has created a fine piece of pottery or turned a canvas into a masterpiece. To rival a fifty-year-old dusty stuffed deer head or an imported production painting on black velvet is as stimulating and inspiring as watching a bear hibernate. These potpourri fairs can be a waste of your time, talent, and money and should be avoided unless you know the people attending are interested in buying genuine crafts and are not just bargain hunters and junk collectors.

It is better if you can get into a juried show. In such a show, a panel of experts associated with gallery, museum, or artists' association screen samples or slides of works of all potential exhibitors. Each piece is judged on a variety of points, such as originality, technique, and command over materials. Competition is stiff. If your work is not accepted, just remember the next panel of judges will probably have a different set of guidelines. Don't change your work to please a jury. Rather, keep looking until you find a jury that your work pleases. One artist recalls her experience with juried shows. A three-man panel, after a lengthy deliberation over her innovative abstract oils, decided to vote against accepting the works. The following month the same three judges sitting on another panel for a different show accepted the identical abstract paintings. As she puts it, "You can't feed a cat romaine when it wants roast. I've learned each judge is different and the same judge will view every show differently. If my work loses out at one exhibit, it will win in at the next." She admits, though, that even now rejections are tough on the ego.

Since juried shows guarantee, to some extent, a more pleasant environment for displaying your items, the exhibitors' fee might be higher than in an open show, and the public may be charged a gate fee. But these shows have a faithful following and are well attended, which means an excellent chance of doing well. Generally, doing well means selling $200 to $250 each day for the duration of the show. It's entirely possible to gross several thousand dollars in just a few days. Anything under $200 daily might mean you've picked the wrong show for your products, the time of year was bad, weather was uncooperative, or the products were overpriced. Don't be discouraged by one or two bad shows.

Michale Rener, a talented midwestern wire sculptor, after a few disappointments, learned which shows are profitable for his products. On a rare occasion he may pick a "slow mover," but nothing so financially disastrous as in the beginning. For the past several years now he's been selling strictly through mall shows and has earned enough to support a family of six. He's learned to discriminate wisely, and you will too.

Some fairs have a theme, and participants are asked to dress in appropriate costumes. America's bicentennial celebration sparked interest in the life and handwork of America's early settlers. Although these shows focus on an era, other crafts (or arts) not related to the theme are usually accepted. A fair of this nature can be fun and provide a refreshing change from the mall show. But don't go overboard by investing all your potential earnings into dressing like Daniel Boone or Martha Washington.

You may have heard about trade shows being held in New York or Los Angeles. Unless you can mass produce your products in enormous quantity and are willing to pay an exorbitant space rental fee, steer clear of these mammoth, mad-house productions. On the other hand, your time may be well spent attending some of the smaller wholesale shows in which you sell solely to shop owners or chain store managers. Even if you sell to shops now, a wholesale show could be very worthwhile. Having prices pat, product line organized, and production capabilities figured in advance will prevent stumbling over answers when a buyer asks questions.

If you are unable to be away from home any length of time, consignment shows may be your answer. Because the products are sold by a professional salesperson, they do not require your presence. You just label each item with your name, item number, and price and make an itemized list, in triplicate, for your records and the salesperson's information. You may find this arrangement frustrating, though, because you have no say in how your products are displayed and do not receive first-hand public reaction to your crafts. Many artisans find that consignment shows produce reams of paperwork and are not very lucrative.

Participating in any show will help your products gain exposure. And even if you're a seasoned craftsperson, this approach can be an effective way of testing new products.

Another advantage of selling through shows is that shop owners often attend looking for new products, and yours might be just what they want. Other show directors attend also, hoping to find qualified artisans they can invite to an up-and-coming event. One of the nicest features that goes with show participation is that you'll have an opportunity to talk with other artisans from various parts of the country and make new friends.

On occasion, you may be asked to "perform" for the customers. If that word conjures a Fred Astaire and Ginger Rogers dance routine, don't become alarmed. What's expected of you is a demonstration in clay throwing, basket weaving, flower making, or whatever your particular craft is. Of course, some crafts do not lend themselves well to demonstration because of the lack of facilities or potential hazards. An example is metal sculpturing that requires heavy arc-welding equipment. Performing your specialty is a great attention-getter, but unless you have an assistant who can explain what you're doing, take orders, and watch that no one pockets an item without paying for it, demonstrating can be a hindrance. An alternative to a live performance would be step-by-step photos with a brief description of the process. Sales may not increase because of the display, but it will give customers a better appreciation of your work and products, and teach them something about the crafts industry in general.

When you're not demonstrating or talking with your neighbor, you will be selling. Making a sale requires more than plopping down the items and sitting back waiting for the rush of eager patrons. Most people are fascinated by artists and handmade crafts. To them you represent a special breed of free spirit. They're curious about you and your work. Don't disappoint your customers; talk with them. It doesn't matter that your free spirit hovers for hours over the workbench or that your independence ends at brushing your own teeth. By talking (not boasting) with a customer about yourself, the products, where you work, you're making contact that just might net you a sale.

Don't underestimate the power of a friendly manner. One of my friends who knows nothing about crafts was recently asked to relieve a potter for an hour so she could grab lunch. The pottery was slow-selling, and the exhibitor thought my friend could do little damage. When the potter returned, she was astonished to find her temporary fill-in had sold over $110 worth of pottery. My friend's bubbling personality, pleasant speaking manner, and genuine interest in the customers had outshined her lack of knowledge of the craft. She warmed and wooed the people into buying. Those she did not sell were given a big thank-you and a business card. Several sales came after the show because of the impression my friend had made and the aid of the business card.

This illustrates the importance of having a large supply of business cards handy to distribute to potential customers. They need not be expensive. Any small paper giving your name, the name of the company, address, phone, and your specialty is sufficient. The most successful business card, however, is a warm smile and a pleasant personality.

How you handle money during a sale can mean the difference between a smooth, uneventful transaction and an embarrassing situation. When the customer gives you the money, always acknowledge the amount and repeat the item's price. Lay the currency in a specific spot before giving the change. This will avoid someone saying he gave you a ten and received change for a five.

In most states you must collect sales tax. A tax chart is helpful. If you are attending an out-of-state show, find out what the sales tax is. Rates differ between states, and in some cases, the tax rate varies from one county to the next.

A lot of shoppers carry plenty of charge cards and very little cash. If you exhibit in many shows and sell expensive crafts, you might consider subscribing to a national charge plan like VISA or Master Charge. It's easy to do, and your local bank will assist with the application. There is no enrollment fee; rather, there is a rental charge for each card imprinter, plus a 3 to 5 percent service charge based on sales.

Most expenses incurred because of a show are tax deductible. For this and other reasons, accurate records must be maintained. The financial value of the show can be evaluated after expenses are subtracted from sales. Minor costs, such as telephone calls, newspapers, and packages of snacks, add up as part of the show expense. If you sold $600 in merchandise during a three-day show, and travel and living expenses ran $200, the balance of $400 must cover the cost of manufacturing and your profit. Doing shows, fortunately, gives you a larger profit margin, since the products are being sold at retail prices.

In addition to having a book listing expenses, a sales receipt pad with a sheet of built-in carbon paper will give you the amount of sales. If you're paying the show director a commission, he may want to use your sales record book to tally the commission due him. Generally, though, directors trust your honesty and accept your figures without question. Also, if you keep a record of the names and addresses of your customers, you'll have a mailing list to use in promoting future shows and direct-mail sales.

Don't make a mistake of lowering your prices during a

show to encourage sales. If you're selling to retail stores, one of your customers might take a dim view of having you as his competitor.

What time of year is best to attend a show? Anytime is best when you make money, but there are definitely better "seasons" than others. Pre-Christmas shows take place from October through mid-December. January through March are slow, and most artisans use those months filling orders for after-Christmas delivery and/or building up stock. Summer is another busy time. Outdoor shows are popular because they make nice family outings. Any show taking place before Easter, Mother's Day, Father's Day, Sweetest Day, and graduations provides good reasons for spending money on gifts. And don't overlook the June bride, who may find a handcrafted lamp or vase a very special gift.

Getting ready for a show can be a head-scratching, frantic, "Did I forget anything?" ordeal. A checklist will prevent leaving the husband and kids on the front steps as you drive the bulging van away. In addition to packing the merchandise and your family, the sales supplies, personal items, and display equipment have to fit somewhere. Make an inventory of the merchandise you're taking to the show. Keep it simple by using a single letter or number code that corresponds with the label on the items. You can use this list to determine which items were sold and if anything was stolen or broken.

You'd probably like to take everything you've made to the fair, but experience proves that certain merchandise does better at some shows than others, and a good variety of products and prices from which to choose is your best bet.

Sales supplies to pack should include business cards, simple brochures, sales book, sales tax chart, inventory checklist, a couple of sharp pencils or pens, a lockable cash box with plenty of change, order forms, packaging material (boxes, bags, pins, scissors, tape, string), and the charge card imprinter and receipts.

Too many show beginners and a few long-time patrons sometimes forget to box some personal items. Everyone's needs differ, but there are certain basic things to take. Comfortable clothing is a must. It should be casual and fit the role of a craftsperson. Think of a leather worker dressed in a tweed business suit. It makes as much sense as wearing a Christian Dior evening gown to a hoedown.

Mother Nature is capricious, and although it isn't nice, loves to fool weather experts. So be prepared for anything from sun to snow, especially if the fair is to be held outside. That includes packing sunglasses, large-brimmed hat, rain gear, awnings, umbrella, boots, and sweater. Ask about inside shelter should there be a chance of rain. If none can be provided, a plastic tarp with poles and ropes for securing will protect your display from a summer downpour. Take beverages, food, and any medication (like headache pills). And, unless you plan to be on your feet all day, bring a chair.

By now there is very little room left in your vehicle, and the display unit still has to be packed. You may think trying to feed another item through the car door will be as easy as pushing an anchor through a keyhole. For this reason, the display should come apart in sections and take no more to assemble and dismantle than fingers, a nail file, and the heel of your shoe. The folding card table is the most universal display apparatus. An attractive cloth draped to the floor will accent your crafts and provide out-of-sight storage space. The rest of the display can be constructed of lightweight, inexpensive material, such as corrugated cardboard, pine, styrofoam panels, balsa wood.

The display unit's shape need not be limited to the conventional L- or U-shaped booth. It can be a triangle made out of wood stock or paper tubes tied with rope, or a pyramid rising from various sizes of boxes or round fiberboard ice cream containers. It can be a rectangular design created from shipping crates. Hinged screens provide a backdrop for the booth which can be easily rearranged to make a dressing room if you sell garments. A circular wall of fabric suspended from tubing that's attached to a rigid wall is another possiblity for providing a fitting space.

Choose background materials to offset your products. Light objects, such as silver jewelry, display well against black velvet. Rustic backgrounds, such as cedar shingles, stained pine boards, and burlap, are excellent for pottery, macrame, rya rugs, and weavings. Using common materials in uncommon ways will add individual flare to your display. Old buckets to hold porcelain flowers, sewer tile to display sculpture, curtain rods to hang paintings, chains to show off tie-dyed scarfs are just a few examples.

Lighting is important, too, so considerable planning is needed. Fire marshalls take their jobs seriously and insist all wiring meet local codes. Perhaps there is sufficient lighting at the show. However, if more is required, a portable unit with an extension cord should be available. Battery-powered lights are an answer if no electrical outlets are accessible at the show.

When displaying your products, design in maximum security, with minimum ostentatiousness, to prevent theft. Place the inexpensive or larger items in front and group the higher-priced and smaller products closer to you so that you can watch them. If you suspect someone has pocketed an object without paying for it, confront him. If this doesn't work, or he walks away before you have a chance to say something, find a security guard or show promoter. But first, get someone to watch your booth, or you may come back to a cleaned-off counter by help-yourselfers. It's more likely, however, your losses will be discovered at the end of the show during an inventory check, when it's too late to do anything but become upset.

One last suggestion. The temptation for some artisans to use every hole in the pegboard and every inch of the table is overwhelming. Resist this temptation, or the finished look will be cluttered, busy, and unappealing. What you want is an attractive display, so keep it simple.

After five fourteen-hour days, the arts and crafts show is finally over. Your feet hope you'll make better use of your seat, your stomach aches for wholesome meals, and your back will never be the same. Now is the time, with everything fresh in your mind, to evaluate the experience. How much of what did you sell? What were your total expenses? Did you like the way the show was organized, and did it run smoothly? What complaints or praises do you have? Would you attend this show again, and if so, what would you do differently? Keep your notes in a binder for future reference. When the following year's entry blank arrives, your notes will tell you whether to go or say no.

With all the pluses, you will have to consider the dimmer side of being a participant for an arts and crafts exhibition. First, a lot of time is consumed packing, unpacking, traveling, setting up, and attending the show. Only after doing a couple of fairs will you be able to determine if the time spent is justified by the sales made, and if you can keep up with the production in between shows. Second, if the show is out of town, the expenses for travel, lodging, and food can multiply quicker than two rabbits in love. Finally, there is no such thing as a "sure" show. Many factors, such as a bad location, time of year, weather, and the mood of the public, can play an important role in whether or not you'll be successful. Sometimes you might return home loaded with more unsold merchandise than hard-earned cash. In most cases, though, you will leave the show with most of the merchandise sold and palatable profit.

It's possible to avoid some of these drawbacks by designing and directing your own show. Feature just your crafts in your home, studio, the front lawn, or a borrowed section of city sidewalk. You will have to do some advertising in the local newspapers and artists' magazines, at colleges and community centers, and by flyers left at neighborhood stores and churches. Try to keep advertising costs low, but be sure to include dates, time, location, and descriptions of the items to be sold. The first couple of one-person shows may be disappointing, but as you and your works become known, attendance and sales will pick up.

Whether you attend a show or do your own, the experience can be personally, professionally, and financially rewarding. And you will perpetuate a rich and timeless tradition started centuries ago by artisans clad in animal hides, living in the hollows of mountains.

CHAPTER SIX

Marketing Techniques

Doing it all—design, produce, sell, and deliver—is enough to undo the best of us. Like pregnancy, it's a fine experience, yet few of us would like to go through it every year. Unlike pregnancy, there are ways to get others to carry part of your load.

Most craftspeople, never really at ease in the marketing arena, look longingly to the day when they can either sell everything they produce through one major chain buyer (more dream than reality), or to the more feasible prospect of hiring a sales representative (known also as a sales agent or manufacturer's representative). But bear in mind that since commissions received from sales are the agent's livelihood, crafts beginners and low-production artisans are gingerly considered. However, once your crafts are established and orders begin to saunter in, agents' interest perks, and, in some instances, they will approach you. One can't help feel a kinship to the fabled Little Red Hen. It is only after you do all the work and have some measure of success that they would like a share of the profits.

But don't be discouraged. To a craft manufacturer, an honest, effective, reputable sales agent is worth every penny of his commission, which averages 15 percent of the wholesale price, but can range between 10 percent for crafts frequently reordered and 30 percent for harder-to-sell, slower-moving items. When analyzing the cost of your product, include the agent's commission. This is a legitimate business expense and comes under production costs.

One of the best ways to find a representative is through the buyers you deal with, as well as the store managers and owners. Other crafts manufacturers with products diverse from yours and crafts organizations are also good sources for personal recommendations. If these methods do not work, the local Chamber of Commerce might have a sales organizations list for your vicinity. Another approach is to advertise in the newspaper or trade journals and magazines. Displaying a want ad for an agent at your next crafts exhibit might prove worthwhile, since sales representatives are faithful followers of arts and crafts shows. The larger metropolitan cities have trade centers where regional national giftware and apparel shows are held. Usually, distributors set up offices at these functions and should be able to provide the names of sales agents in your territory.

If it takes too long to find the right agent for you, or even spur one's interest, console yourself that good representatives are busy and may not find it feasible to add your line. In most instances though, if your items have a fair track record and complement (but not compete with) those presently being handled by the agent, he will gladly take them on. After all, he's in the business to make money, as you are, and a representative will seldom pass a chance to increase his income. As one New York agent put it, "I'm not so quick to turn my head without first looking to see what I'm turning away from. The last time I did cost me a bundle. I refused to handle a small smoking kit because I saw no potential, even though the manufacturer had a fair amount of success selling them herself. Someone else picked it up and in the first year tripled his commissions."

Once you have found a manufacturer's representative, several basic but important points should be covered and thoroughly understood. He should supply the names and addresses of at least three credit references and several artisans or companies he is selling for or has represented in the past. Too often a tale of woe is told by the unsuspecting crafts manufacturer who had both the agent and merchandise disappear without a trace.

Some agents prefer to enter into a signed contract relationship, while others are more informal, and a mere handshake closes the deal. Should you be presented with what appears to be a fifty-page, unabridged legal document, it would be best to have an attorney review it first, unless, of course, you're Perry Mason moonlighting in crafts.

Contract or handshake, you should have in written form what is expected from each of you to prevent any misunderstandings and problems. For example, the agent may want evidence and assurance you'll be able to produce what he sells and maintain the quality. You'll want to set a minimum volume of sales, know what percentage of commission he wants, how and when it will be paid, and if there are any other costs in addition to the commission, such as a fee for displaying your items at his showroom, if there is one, or having product flyers printed, and any advertising costs. If there are such additional costs, figure them into the total cost of producing your product.

Also cover the number of samples for each item the agent will need, and whether the wholesale price of the products will be charged against his or her commissions or memo-billed until they have been returned. Next, agree on how often orders are to be forwarded, if you want the agent to do the credit reference checking of the stores, and who will handle the problem of a late payment, should it occur. Perhaps you may wish to be able to refuse an order. Include this in your written agreement with the understanding the agent will be informed within a specified time. On occasion a shop will return a shipment. Decide how the deduction, if any, of the commission will be handled, though it is best to pay the representative commissions only when the invoices have been paid by the retailer. One anxious-to-cooperate crafts producer paid his sales agent commissions within thirty days after shipment, regardless of whether or not the invoice had been paid. He soon realized most of his accounts went forty-five days or longer before he saw the store's check. Consequently, too much of his "manufacturing money" was tied up in commissions.

Often, a sales agent has a certain territory and wants to be the exclusive representative of your products in that area. He may expect to receive his commission on sales made in his territory, even if the sales were made through other means. Get this point resolved because a business relationship can sour more quickly than milk mixed with vinegar when it comes to a sales and commission disagreement.

Assuming you both have survived the written agreement, and still want to work together, supply the representative with every bit of material you have about your products and business. The better equipped he is, the more effective his selling will be. Your "salesman kit" should include multiple copies of price lists, order forms, product information sheets, brochures, credit check forms, photos, and samples.

When an order comes in, it is a sound business practice to send a confirmation to the shop. You will be letting the store know not only that the order has been received, but that it is correct and what the approximate shipping date will be. Always ship within the time stated and with the quality of the product equal to or surpassing that of the samples. At the time you invoice the store, forward a copy to your agent. This will keep you and the agent informed of sales made and possible commissions due.

By working closely with your representative, you will be kept on top of any new wares or trends in the market and the buyer's reactions to your products. The agent may even have a money-making suggestion for a unique product. Listen to him. Not only is he a reflection of you and your crafts, but being exposed daily to the consumer-goods market, he is an excellent sounding board. Should any problems arise with production, late shipments, or collection, let the agent know. It is easier to keep him advised of your affairs than a buyer one hundred miles away.

If, however, you find you and the agent are not compatible, your relationship may be terminated by mutual agreement. The agent may then begin selling a competitive line of products to the same people who were buying your crafts. Instead of threatening to weave him into a horse blanket, keep the momentum of sales by wholesaling to those retail stores yourself.

Either through your own past efforts or the agent's you should have a fair-sized list of buyers, and once your products have been established in several outlets, you can concentrate on the production.

But, you say, this is your first attempt at wholesaling and you have no established outlets. Then there is a lot of leg work, door knocking, and time juggling ahead of you. Being your own middleman initially is like sitting at both ends of the seesaw. As your activity in selling goes up, the time spent on manufacturing heads down. If you are a creature of midnight creativity, producing by night and selling by day may just suit you. In any event, your persistence and hard work will be paid for by the higher percentage of return on the sales, since the step between you and the retailer has been eliminated.

Before even thinking about seeing a buyer, though, plan how to show your products most effectively. Successfully selling your crafts to a buyer is 40 percent creation and 60 percent presentation. Most of us indulge in the fleeting daydreams of plopping down our creations before our very first all-eyes, all-ears buyer and being given a blanket order for "all you can make of everything." It doesn't usually work this way. Recently, a talented husband and wife team manufactured a very clever and attractive mood lamp. They offered several different lighting effects, but to keep manufacturing simple, all the lamps looked the same. A great deal of time and money went into stocking a sizable supply, but, because funds were limited, no brochures or pamphlets were printed for distribution to the buyers. The young couple had to carry with them one sample of each model, and ten models were offered.

If they left their samples with one buyer, the next buyer wasn't too interested in a verbal and hand-gestured description. The couple decided, after nightly feet soaks and cooperative backrubs, that thinning the bank account for a product flyer would help ease the mounting calluses and increase the salability of the lamps.

Also, buyers could use the pamphlet, which contained a picture of the products, quantity pricing, delivery schedules and conditions, payment terms, and the manufacturer's name, address, and phone number, as a convenient means of placing future orders. As unique and desirable as a product may be, buyers cannot possibly remember the dozens of items they see daily and the statistics that go with them.

Next, do some store detective work. As you did when searching out a shop to consign your first crafted items, snoop around to see where your goods might best fit. You certainly wouldn't think of showing a leather-fringed jacket next to a silk nightgown. Nor would a hand-blown vase fit in with camping lanterns. Take note of the way products similar to yours are displayed, paying special attention to the quality and price. Keep in mind that the retailer will mark up the wholesale price 100 percent. Therefore, if you sell a macrame handbag to the store for $6, the bag will retail for $12.

You can obtain the name and home-base location of the buyer from the department manager. Because of the buyer's hectic, catch-me-between-stores schedule, always call, do not write, the buyer or her assistant for an appointment. This is your first contact with the buyer, so strive for a good impression. Rehearse, out loud if necessary, how you'll get your specific points of interest across to the buyer. Basics, such as your name, particular skill, description of the products, and appointment request, of course, should be covered.

On the appointed day, checklist your carrying case. Are all samples properly tagged with model numbers and prices? Do you have printed material describing the crafts, models offered, quantity pricing, minimum order, sizes, colors, delivery schedules, and payment terms? Think positively, and take along an order book and pen or pencil.

Make sure everything is clean, neat, and in order, including you. One Maryland buyer told me that she missed the whole sales pitch by a silversmith because she couldn't draw her attention away from his "lived-in" appearance. Consequently, he went away without getting an order.

If your first appointment with a buyer makes you feel more like a three-day-old salad than a designer, you're not alone. A friend of mine who is a very talented weaver had a disastrous first encounter with a buyer. "I was so nervous," she said, "that I perspired all over my samples, and if that weren't enough, I babbled incessantly about my entire life history. I was a nightmare out of *True Confessions*. I think the buyer placed an order just to save her sanity and get me out the door."

Although we all may not be so extreme, we can expect some "sellers jitters" at first. Be assured that each contact should get easier and go more smoothly. Buyers are not the unreasonable, cold, and calculating creatures we conjure up in our moments of panic. In fact, most buyers are very receptive if you have something interesting and high quality to offer. But they are busy people, so be prepared to give a concise and informative product demonstration while highlighting a few interesting facts about the products, yourself, and the business. When you've convinced the buyer to place an order, don't forget to cover payment terms, and if applicable, to get a few credit references. Also, don't assume that one order will ensure a continuous, long-range selling agreement. In fact, don't assume anything.

Sometimes a buyer will ask you to leave your samples overnight or for a few days so that his or her associates can see them. Don't do it. There is a practice among some disreputable store managements known as "purloining." While they have your samples, the items are scrutinized and dissected, then returned to you with a "thank you, but, sorry, we just can't use them." Months later a similar, perhaps cheaper, version of your item can be found in the store. It is a frustrating and humiliating experience. Avoid the possibility. Offer instead to return another day when you can show your products to the associates yourself. Most stores, and their buyers, fortunately, would not take advantage of you, but just be alert that some may try.

Perhaps avoiding buyers completely sounds like a good idea, but you don't want to go back to having your products handled by a sales agent. Then a wholesale distributor might be just the answer. The distributor is an individual or company which acts as the middleman between you and the retailer. Unlike a manufacturer's representative, who just *represents* your crafts, the distributor *buys* them from you at a discount of one third off the wholesale price. There are some definite advantages to this marketing technique. First, your bookkeeping is simplified because you would most likely sell to one or two distributors instead of a dozen or so retail shops. Second, the distributor will pay you before the merchandise is resold. Third, once the merchandise is delivered, storage of the products and shipment to retailers are his responsibility. Next, a large firm can generally reach a greater variety of markets and buyers than you or a single sales agent can. Last, the necessary but burdensome task of checking credit references, and collection problems are no longer your concern.

Exclusivity of your products might be one of the distributor's conditions. It can be advantageous if the orders produced keep you at the workbench, but not so desirable if you have to reject other potentially good prospects, such as hiring your own salesperson.

Unlike an agent or distributor, a salesperson is your employee. He would receive a base salary or draw against commissions and any company benefits, such as vacation, sick days, and health insurance. Being his employer, you would have more direct control over how his time is spent and his actions in the field. Of course, your production would have to be at a level to justify this added operating expense. But hiring a salesperson can generate a lot of business through the efforts of a loyal, hard-working employee.

There is a breed of "product promoter" who appear to be just as faithful and sales-oriented as your own employee. These slick operators are very professional and offer an impressive mail campaign to a worldwide market. For an exorbitant price of $3,000 or more, usually payable in no more than six monthly installments, you will be assured of large-volume sales within a specific time, which generally falls after you have paid the entire fee. In conversations with two Chicago manufacturers, an Ohio crafts producer, and a Washington artisan who had tried this marketing technique, not one had any of their products sold. They had all paid their "dues" and received nothing but blue-sky pep talks and endless reassurances that "it takes time to reach just the right market for your product." Four years later these four people, and countless more, are still waiting for the low cloud cover to clear.

Never pay an organization or individual a "promotional fee" to move your products, no matter how encouraging, persuasive, and enthusiastic the promotor may be. Stick with the sales agent, sell them yourself, go with a distributor, or hire your own salesperson. Any of these wholesaling methods will work to move your crafts items out of the cellar to the crafts-consuming public.

CHAPTER SEVEN

From Post to Profits

Direct mail sales are as much a part of Americana as the image of a Sears and Roebuck catalog in an outhouse. The shopping spree A. Montgomery Ward started in 1872 when he mailed his first thin catalog has grown into a $50-billion-a-year industry. Everything from airplanes to zippers can be purchased through the mails. Americans accept and appreciate the convenience of direct mail purchasing. In an earlier age this may have been explained by the great distances between rural families and the goods marketplace, but today there is no real explanation except for a long-standing tradition and trust in the integrity of postal system and merchants alike.

Postal sales can be made to order for craftspeople. It takes your work out of the confines of your local area. You can sell from a basement workshop or kitchen table any time of the day or night. Live in an urban highrise or retreat to the backwoods. Just as long as there is a cleared path to a post office, you're in business. There is also a tremendous degree of flexibility in sales by mail. You can place ads in newspapers or magazines, send flyers directly to potential customers' homes, or distribute a catalog alone or with other craftspeople. With all of these methods the US Post Office acts as your ally.

Yet mail order sales are not for every craftsperson. Even a modest mailing of a few thousand brochures can cost several hundred dollars. And unless you have reason to be confident that your product has mass appeal, you could end up not receiving a single order for your efforts.

Although there is no absolute standard for what sells by mail, experience has provided some general guidelines. Uniqueness is, as always in crafts, a first priority. It must be a design item that is desirable to a large number of people, yet one which is not readily available in local stores or in a Sears–Roebuck catalog. The item must be compact and light enough to make mailing economical, yet sturdy enough to survive the ten-thumbed handling by postal clerks. Price is paramount in direct mail sales. People are reluctant to send a check for hundreds of dollars for something they've never seen, but won't think twice in sending for a $2 item. In general, a $20 limit per item is most realistic until a mail order operation has developed enough public trust to chance big-ticket items.

You've got a head start if your item is one that has appeal as a gift. Even in hard times, we expect and give presents. That knowledge made Harry and David, founders of the large and thriving mail order fruit business in Oregon, persist even in the middle of the Depression. They appealed to businessmen to order gift boxes from them, and a unique idea caught on. Even as they grew, they kept a personal touch, and one happy pear eater led to another.

Knowing your customer and how to reach her or him directly is the key to making money through the mails. Display ads in national magazines or even local newspapers are expensive and, for the number of people reached, generally unproductive. Contacting people whom you know to be interested in your craft and who actually buy such items is the way of getting the greatest return on every dollar you invest in marketing. Display ads, however, are important because they are a method of weeding out your audience. The people who respond to your broad-based ad and buy once will likely buy again. So all you have to do is keep their names and addresses, and next time you can appeal to them directly, eliminating the need for a publication advertisement.

In compiling names and addresses of sure-sales customers, you're building a mailing list. The better your list is, the bigger your profits will be. So mailing lists are of central importance to the direct mail businessperson. There are two ways to get a good list. First, you can go the ad route that we've mentioned to build your own. That takes time and money, yet it is highly productive. Second, and more common, you can rent or buy lists. Most direct mail people do both. They buy lists to get started, and then build their own as the names of customers come in on order forms.

Len Carlson, the founder of Los Angeles' Sunset House, advises beginners to rent a competitor's list. This doesn't necessarily mean a direct competitor. If you're a maker of coal jewelry, you might not find a fellow coal-jewelry maker willing to share his list with you, but a weaver may consider you no threat to his business and be delighted to make the extra money by renting you his list. Also, established mail order houses often rent their lists. The middleman to contact is a mailing list broker. Look in phone directories of large cities to locate them and request brochures.

Study the offerings of various brokers; prices vary according to the type of list you need. The names can even be purchased on gummed labels so that you can simply peel and stick or hand them over to a printer to affix by machine. It is possible to sample a few thousand names from a large (twenty-thousand-name) list, but it is less expensive to rent a smaller list, one with four thousand or so names. The best lists name people who have made recent purchases.

Your most productive list will probably be the one you eventually compile yourself. It will consist of former customers, their friends, and those who have shown interest in your work possibly at fairs or shows. If you're starting from scratch, a little imagination will get you going. A young Wisconsin couple operating on a very limited budget collected names by asking friends for their Christmas card lists.

Keep a watchful eye on your customers so that you will have "clean" lists. This means weeding out those who have died and updating addresses. And make sure the ones you rent have been cleaned recently. A reputable mailing list company will stand behind its lists.

Keep precise records. They not only save you postage, but help determine how effective your lists are. Maintain a card file of those who have purchased items and those who have made inquiries, complete with dates. The percentage of sales from mailing lists varies greatly. Returns may range from one tenth of 1 percent to 2 percent. Careful pruning and cultivation of a list might ultimately bring a yield of 5, or even 10 percent. With this in mind, you shouldn't put out the kiln fire or use the loom for kindling wood if your initial mailing is a no-profit venture, particularly if your craft is low-priced. Recognize that this is one discouraging aspect of mail order selling. Initial costs can be high, but as you hone in on your market, the banker will start speaking to you again.

You can further refine your list by noting in your files

which geographic areas bring the most sales and aiming your money at the most productive target.

Getting your advertisement into the right hands is half the sales job; the other half is convincing the recipient that you have something he or she wants. Your mailing flyer or brochure must be showy enough to attract the reader's attention, yet not so flashy that it is immediately categorized as junk mail and tossed out with the garbage. Display your crafts with pictures, but use enough written material to explain features, price, and quality. As a craftsperson, you might also want to say something about yourself to add the personal touch.

You don't have to be a polished writer to produce a successful mail order piece. In fact, it may help not to be, since you won't be tempted to flower the prose in typical ad-man style. The most important point is to tell your prospective customer *why* your craft is worth having. You are expected to brag, but don't oversell your merchandise. In the long run, it will injure your credibility and kill your chances of repeat sales. Be direct, honest, and brief. Have someone else go over your copy to see how many words are unnecessary and can be cut. Also, you'll want to mention as many of your products in each mailing item as possible. The more choices you give a customer, the greater your odds of making a sale or even a several-item sale from the one contact.

Ad agencies will be happy to design the mailer for you, but they will be equally delighted to bill you more than most craftspeople can afford. You don't really need them. With photo typesetting and modern printing techniques, anyone can lay out an attractive advertisement. Instant printing shops and small printers have all the equipment for setting your words into any number of designs and with a wide variety of type faces and headline sizes. The promotion pictures you've used to sell to chain store buyers and galleries can be included with little or no reproduction needed. The small printer can also give you three-color printing, but if your budget is like most craftspeople's, you'll want to stick to two-color or black and white.

In the advertising business there are no hard-and-fast rules. You can apply the creativity you've used in your craft to molding an attractive ad. Looking at ads others have used in a variety of magazines, with special attention to crafts ads, naturally, can give you ideas. But there is no formula for success. Most beginners will want to try several different approaches with each mailing or publication ad until a winning combination of words and art is achieved. The rule is, if it sells, use it again. Eventually you'll come up with the right format for your work and forever after will be able to merely plug in new information, pictures, and prices to update your selling piece.

The same words and pictures can be used in a variety of ad media. You can have the material from your one-page leaflet reset or cut down to use in a newspaper ad, or expanded to produce a brochure. Once you've gone through the trouble of producing a single mailing piece or ad, you have the makings for an entire advertising campaign.

Your first advertising will probably appear in local newspapers. Finding the right one isn't difficult. Go to the library and scan recent editions of the papers published in your area to find a spot where your creations will be exposed to an appreciative audience. The publications you'll want are those that carry accounts from the better department stores, have feature stories on the arts, and that other crafters use. No one paper may have all of this, and in others only Sunday magazine sections may meet your standards. But pick the ones that come as close as possible to reflecting the high quality of your work. A publication with ads by small, exclusive shops indicates a good choice for any craftsperson. If the discount houses buy more space than the better department stores, move on to another publication. The quality of your work is affected by the company it keeps on a page of ads. At least that's how the public sees it, and that is, after all, what counts.

Living in a rural area may limit your choices. But sticking to the hometown daily isn't all bad for starters. You'll get a feel for working with the press, a field test for your product, and a trial run for your ad without too much expense.

A brochure or flyer that has been used for other promotion is probably serviceable for a newspaper ad. If you're going from color to black and white, choose the print carefully. Newsprint is a poor quality paper that shows only the strongest contrast well. It is sometimes hard to judge contrast from a color print. To further complicate matters, weavings, candles, and small pieces of jewelry tend to get lost in a black and white photo, especially if it has been reduced in size.

You might also want to place your ad in a magazine or two. Many magazines have a section at the back devoted to craft items, kits, stationery, and other novelty items for home or personal use. Guidelines for choosing a magazine or one of the larger national newspapers to advertise in should be the same as those for placing your craft in a particular shop or store. You'll want to bring your craft to the most interested buyer in the least competitive setting at the most reasonable cost.

Another trip to the library is in order. Larger metropolitan libraries will have copies of The *Standard Periodical Directory* or the *Ayer Directory of Publications*. *Standard Periodical* contains information on more than sixty thousand publications. The listings are done by subject and include all publication information plus the cost of a one-time black and white full-page ad. The *Ayer Directory* lists newspapers published throughout the United States, the line rate for black and white ads, and the one-time rate for specified magazine ads. Consumer, business, technical, trade, and farm magazines are the only ones carried by *Ayer*. Both publications list circulation numbers, which are essential if you're to get your money's worth. A craftsperson with limited funds trying to reach a large market is better off paying for an ad which reaches five million readers than buying space that will reach only five thousand readers. Some advertisers exclusively play the readers-per-dollar game. They simply calculate cost per thousand readers (space rate divided by circulation), then go with the lowest rate that reaches the most people. The readers-per-dollar approach, however, ignores the specialized nature of a publication and its readership. Given identical rates, a magazine circulated to two thousand wealthy people is, in fact, a more likely bargain if you're selling yachts than a two-million circulation magazine that goes to laborers. Obviously, the appropriateness of the readership to your product is as vital, perhaps far more vital, than a simple rate-per-thousand "bargain" is.

Always spend time investigating the magazine's clientele. Reading the publication is one way; another is to find a recent copy of *Writer's Market*. This book, published to aid freelance writers in finding suitable markets for their work, describes the readers' interests. This can help the craftsperson, too. If you have leather belts and wicker baskets, you might find a niche in *Field and Stream* among the fishermen and sportsmen. Makers of fine filigree jewelry might opt for *Vogue,* and both specialties have had exposure in *The New Yorker. Writer's Market* also tells writers when to submit seasonal material. This information is a clue to ad placers. A magazine typically is put together three to six months ahead of newsstand delivery. If you wish to advertise your holiday crafts works, copy must be submitted by April, or May at the latest, for fall exposure. Furniture maker Brad Otterman says, "In any given year I have my latest designs tried and marketable right after the holidays. It's kind of a backwards situation. While everyone is shopping, caroling, and cheering the New Year, my timetable says design, market, and produce." Brad places his ads in February, March, and April to give the browser a chance to mull over a purchase before order-ing. Therefore, to gear up for an autumn campaign, you should query the advertising account manager, study the price rates, submit your ad copy, and establish your account as soon after the first of the year as possible. It takes time to communicate by mail, and you'll want time to study all the options.

Both newspapers and magazines offer bargain plans. Investi-gate these possibilities. It may get you more advertising for your money. If experience has shown, for example, that November advertisements account for most of your business, you may be able to arrange a discounted rate for a regular November commitment, then limit your advertising to that one most productive mouth. Because of the variety of crafts that can be sold through mail order, every ad space agreement is unique. This is a real horse trader's business, so if you're not afraid of bickering over price with the ad space salespeople, you can work outstanding deals.

Whether it's to go in a newspaper or magazine, fact-pack your ad. Try to convey a lot of information in a tight space. With a sketch or photograph you've already delivered a thousand words. You also need a few words to the reader concerning the address, shipping and postage costs, if any, and the guarantee. Choices of color, size, or design, and, of course, the price should be there too. Some ads include an order form. This increases the cost of the ad, but it sometimes pays off because it's handy. Other extras might be your telephone number for local orders and a code number to let you know which paper "delivered" the response. For instance, if you placed ads in both the *Dundaldee Daily* and the *Worker's Weekly,* you might label your ads DD-100 for the former and WW-100 for the latter. If the DD orders surpass the WW's, you know where to place your next advertising dollars.

Some craftspeople specify a four- to six-week delivery notice in their ads. It isn't necessary. The Federal Trade Commission requires a thirty-day delivery period on goods ordered through the mail, so although saying you might tarry a little is nice, it won't get you off the hook with the FTC if complaints are made. (Notifying each customer in writing after an order is received will buy you time and is approved by the FTC.)

Ad placement is critical in catching the reader's eye. Studies show that the average American immediately looks to the upper right-hand corner of a page, a habit acquired by reading newspapers, where the biggest story appears in the high right-hand spot. Insist on a forward-facing ad, one which is on the right when the reader turns to that page. You may have to pay a premium for such exposure, but it's invaluable.

If you're into many designs or want to market more comprehensively, you might want to try cataloging your craft. Catalogs are a natural outlet for mail order sales. What will it do for you? First, it is armchair exposure. People browse through catalogs more carefully than they do magazine ads and often pass them on to friends and neighbors. It's quite different from the passing glance you get at a large show. And second, your product is more than shown. It is put into the hands of a potential buyer. He or she can look at it over and over again. Catalog companies have the capital to purchase, rent, or develop the best buyer lists available. Interest is more than casual; it is proven.

There are four ways to become involved in catalog sales. You can wholesale your craft to a mail order business that will retail it through their catalog. You can buy ad space in a craft catalog that sells items similar in quality and price to yours. You can pool your time, talent, and cash with one or several other craftspeople to put together your own catalog. Or, you can shoot for a free ad in a specialty catalog that judges submissions and features only outstanding works.

If choice number one is yours, flip to Chapter Six and review the ins and outs of wholesaling. Beyond that, there are a few additional considerations when the wholesaling is being done through a catalog. Browse through some catalogs. *Artisans and Craftsmen* (a division of Environmental Educators, Inc., 2100 M Street, N.W., Washington, DC 20037) puts together retail catalogs that feature handmade crafts exclusively. They consider all media and display items in a wide price range. They will also feature limited edition craft items, but not one-of-a-kind. *Artisans and Craftsmen* has standards which are rather typical of wholesale catalogs.

A catalog company may want to set the retail price of your

item and have full control over markdowns and sale specials. This is not a rule, however, and it is to your advantage to assert full control over your retail price and discount it at a wholesale rate. Why? If the corner shop sells your miniatures for $1, and the cataloger marks them at $1.50, you're competing against yourself. Set a retail price that reflects a reasonable profit for you. Some use a five-times rule of thumb. Five times the basic cost of materials and production time ensures them a profit when unexpected costs, such as shipping and materials increases, come up after orders have been placed. Because you're working with wholesalers, discount terms are negotiable. Each company will share its own set of guidelines with you. Deciding what is fair and reasonable is a personal decision. You don't want to undersell yourself, but you don't want to put yourself out of competition either. One experience with a company will give you know-how for future negotiations. With the paperwork done you're obligated to produce your craft in quantity, sometimes up to several hundred units. From then on it's easy. You're paid within thirty days of shipment, and the wholesaler covers the expense of photography, printing, and mailing.

The Goodfellow Catalog of Wonderful Things (Box 4520, Berkeley, CA, 94704) is a specialty catalog. From several hundred submissions a panel selects the best in American crafts. This type of catalog seeks to promote excellence in crafts, but also shares the lifestyle, philosophy, and outlook of the individuals involved. In a recent edition six hundred representatives displayed crafts works through photographs. They accept actual items, as well as photographs, for judging and selection. The Goodfellow people will do the photography, but if you do your own, go professional. When you're

being judged from a picture rather than an actual work, it's
to be great.

The Goodfellows are most interested in durable, novel,
high-quality work that gives the catalog an overview of
American crafts and their history. Even if you don't approach
them, this is a catalog worth looking over. It may give you
ideas for one of your own. The tone is "down home" and
personal. The products displayed are not cheap, but not
unreasonable. Even though reproductions are made, the crafts
works have a one-of-a-kind look. And there is variety.
Everything from furniture to candles is included.

There are many smaller catalogs. You'll see them advertised
in sports, home-life, recreation, furniture, family, hobby, and
crafts magazines. They pop up all over. You'll probably spot
an ad for one next time you're waiting at the doctor's office.
Order as many catalogs as you can find that show products like
yours. When they arrive, check them out to see if there is a
logical reason why your craft might fit in well. Send a letter to
the cataloger. Tell him or her why you think his catalog could
use your product. Express a personal interest in their other
products and point out why buyers would want yours. Offer
to send samples, and include pertinent information about size,
color, choices, weight, and price. Use a friendly approach. You
might say something like:

> In your recent *Earth-Time* catalog I noticed many
> unusual Americana items that were not only attractive
> but functional. I have made some straw brooms that
> would fit in well with your "Home and Hearth" section.
> Not only are they decorative, but they're sized for either
> kitchen or hearth use. I'd be happy to send a sample

broom if you'd like to consider it for your mail order business. . . .

Offering to send a sample is a good idea. Enclosing a self-addressed, stamped postcard for reply is better. Often buyers who do not purchase your product will respond with helpful suggestions (a change in color, size, etc.) if a postcard is enclosed. It can't hurt. And a reply means you're at least under consideration. Even if the organizer has a full catalog now, your letter may be filed for the future. The buyer may reply with a request that you contact him at a later date. Keep track of your correspondence and replies.

Selling your product to a mail order cataloger requires an inventory commitment. Catalogs stay in circulation a lot longer than magazines or newspapers do. Orders can come in up to two years after a catalog has been issued. This is more than something to think about. If you're going ahead, let the buyer know you are willing to fill a long-term obligation. Using the broom example, you could say, "I can fill orders from one to twelve dozen on two weeks' notice." This assures the buyer that you are willing to deliver in quantity when buying time comes around.

Catalogs that charge space rates are not usually wholesalers. Here it's just like advertising in a magazine or newspaper. You pay for an ad, receive orders, then do the packing and shipping. These publications deserve the same high-quality presentation that the "free rides" demand. Since photographic services are rarely provided, you'll want to seek the excellence of a professional. This cannot be emphasized too much. Crafts works lend themselves to handling and touching. You'll lose quality even in the best photograph, so don't economize here.

The most costly catalog is one you put together yourself. Even in a brochure you'll want to picture at least a dozen designs. It isn't the number that's so important, but a need for variety. Putting art into print, however, is expensive. Not only do you entail photographic costs, but you must use high-quality paper for print reproduction, which is also heavier and naturally more expensive to fold, staple, and mail. Easing the cost burden by going in with another craftsperson is something to think about. If your crafts are compatible, you might be able to reduce photographic fees by grouping similar items. If you design belt buckles and she tools belts, you've got a likely marriage. In crafts, that is. Other combinations might be candles and candle holders, ceramic pots and macrame hangers, quilts and afghans, stained glass and jewelry. The list goes on and on. The point is to use your artistic sense to pair eye-pleasing combinations.

Whether you've decided to team up with someone or go it alone, make your first stop the printer. It's his job to chart your needs and point you in the direction of a photographer, artist, or writer, if you need one. If you do need a photographer, hunt among your fellow craftspeople. There may be usable talent in your own local organization. Small newspapers often use free-lancers who can do professional work at reasonable prices, and the senior citizens' club may have some excellent hobbyists who can help you out. Fees for a writer can be eliminated if you know your craft and can "talk about it" to a buyer. The most important message goes on the cover. Take care to get it just right. "Crafts Galore" may be too dimestore and "Awl-Work," too obscure. Test out your eye-catcher on a seven-year-old. If she can guess what's inside the booklet without looking and finds it amusing too, you're in. Use it.

Everyone likes to smile, and a cute title asks to be picked up.

The printer's expenses vary with the amount of color you use and the quantity. The more color, the higher the cost; the more catalogs, the less the cost per issue. Shop around, and when you find the best deal, get to work on building stock. The orders will soon roll in.

If your craft would lend itself to construction by beginners, given step-by-step instructions, there's room for you in the kit side of mail order. Any easily-reproduced craft can be marketed as a kit. It's one way of marketing a half-finished project at full cost. To do this, you must satisfy the seven "its": design it, define it, try it, write it, show it, advertise it, sell it.

Designing it as a kit requires breaking the process down into simple, logical steps. You already carry a mental design of the craft you work. Just be sure to start at the beginning. You're dealing with novices who need explicit instruction. If you can detail five or six steps, your chances of sales are better than if you offer a twenty-step package.

Next you'll have to define your terms. Assume your "student" customer knows nothing about the craft. A macrame beginner won't recognize a square knot the first time around, and the beginning needleworker has to know that a French knot is something more than a hairstyle. Include a materials list and a way to tell yickles from zoo-zoos. This can be done by packaging and labeling the pieces that go into the package. Suppose you put a shellcraft cookie jar into kit form. All shells that are used for the lid could go into bag "A." If the design is a progression of rings of shells that go around the jar with the largest shells in the bottom ring and the smallest ones at the top, the shells for each separate ring could be bagged and labeled. Clear definitions will make the buyer comfortable with the materials, and mistakes will be avoided.

Designs and definitions will stand trial when you test the kits. Your jury will be a group of guinea pigs who are not craftspeople. To accurately "try it," your willing workers should represent a cross section of age, sex, and interest groups. If you already teach your craft, you have a ready-made group of testers. Even though you've done a presentation many times, when kit sales are the object, you'll want to make careful note of the steps you've given the class, the kinds of questions they ask, and how their efforts turn out.

If the trial run goes smoothly, write it down. Use simple language and number the steps.

When you're satisfied with your copy, add sketches or photographs to illustrate each basic step and get a photograph or colorful reproduction of the finished product to go on the cover of the kit. It shows the buyer how his or her efforts will come out. This is no place for surprises.

Now double-check your kit. Without any direction from you, a hobbyist should be able to do the project in a short time. Problems such as vague directions, poor materials, or fuzzy sketches must be corrected before production gets underway. Smoothing out the details will go far when it comes to repeat business.

To advertise the kit, start locally. The kit can be the required text if you teach. From there go to magazines, newspapers, and specialty catalogs. The best advertisement, of course, is the reputation of a quality, easy-to-do, well-packaged item that is bought over and over again by pleased customers. If they know who you are by the high standards of your kits, they'll ask for you. Your name (or company name) is important. Let it be visible on the cover and on the reorder form you've tucked inside.

Selling it can be done through free press coverage which is

outlined in Chapter Nine. Arousing the interest of your own community can generate a local pride and word-of-mouth campaign that will keep your order box filled. Sharon Timmons began decorative egg-craft kits that way. She says, "My idea was to make a simple, attractive decoration that would do double duty. My styrofoam kits come with egg shapes, sequins, velvet ribbon, decorative pins, fabric, glue, and a Christmas tree hanger. Folks using the kit can put together an Easter decoration and then hang it on the tree at Christmas. My neighbors thought it was such a cute idea they bought me out before I spent a cent on ads. After an article in the newspaper, my kits sales doubled, and now I received orders from aunts, uncles, and cousins from all over the country."

When it comes to mailing kits or your own handmade creations, it's a bit more complicated than simply dropping them in a mailbox. The federal and local governments have a few things to say about mail order businesses. The Federal Trade Commission is concerned about merchandise that travels across state lines. They have their famous truth-in-advertising statutes and also a less-known thirty-day-delivery ruling. If a thirty-day delivery cannot be met, you must notify the customer in writing and give him the choice of cancelling or waiting another thirty days. A free means of stopping the order must be provided (a post card is fine), and if you don't fill the order within sixty days, the buyer is entitled to a full refund. He may be willing to wait longer. In this case he must notify you in writing. An exception to the thirty-day ruling is with COD orders, because the buyer's money is not tied up. COD, however, is not recommended for craftspeople. With your income already delayed by catalog publication and waiting for orders, you don't need the further worry of waiting for money that isn't sent until after goods are received.

In some cases crafts articles are also regulated by the Food and Drug Administration. The Food, Drug, and Cosmetic Act covers standards of purity, content, and dosage that must be followed. If you use paints or stuff pillows, you may be affected by these codes. Ignorance won't get you off the hook, so check with your local FDA offices, which are listed in the telephone directory, or write to the FDA, Washington, DC 20250, for information pertaining to your particular product.

In addition to federal trade and content regulations, excise taxes affect a few craftspeople. Tobacco, liquor, and firearms top the list. A leather pouch maker who includes a tobacco sample is affected, and so is the gunsmith who makes full-scale reproductions. Liquor rarely becomes a part of a craft, but if you think any of the three are related to the product you market, you must contact the US Treasury Department, 15th Street, N.W., Washington, DC, 20220. Request excise tax information about your product.

You will need to be concerned with local and state sales taxes if you mail within your own state. Check with state and municipal offices and request tax information pertaining to your business.

Licensing and other local regulations vary greatly. You may have to register the name of your business or check out zoning laws to see if you can operate a mail order business from your home. In most cases local governments don't hassle the small businessperson, but because we are a country of individuals, you should check with your own city clerk to keep your record clear of possible violations.

With the legal groundwork covered, your craft neatly catalogued and well advertised, the orders are bound to start coming in. This should please you very much. Your next job is to please the customer by acknowledging the order, packaging it, and shipping it promptly. It sounds simple, but this is where most mail order set-ups fall down.

You can be the exception. Start by using postcards that state when the order was received, the date you expect to ship, and how it will arrive (UPS, US postal service, Air Freight).

You might want to give yourself some leeway for shipping time to avoid raising the ire of impatient customers in case of postal delays. Ann Haggarty is a glassblower whose Indiana residence is, in her words, "near nothin'." She says, "I usually make it in to the post office once a week on Fridays. I assume the service isn't too great anywhere, and out here it seems particularly slow, so when I write to customers, I add a good seven days onto the expected date of delivery. I haven't had a complaint yet." You may not have to go to such extremes if you live "near somethin'," but the point is, customers appreciate knowing you've received their money and when they can expect the goods.

Packing your craft is your next concern. All of your work up until now could be lost if you don't do this well. Even a rag doll can be damaged in transit. Woodwork can scratch, pottery chip, weavings bleed, and silver tarnish. Start from the inside out. Every object in the package must be labeled. According to the American Crafts Council, the label information should include your name, a description of the object, its size, and the number of pieces included. Other information required by the FTC or FDA for use, care, or content should also go on your label. Each tagged item can then be individually wrapped. Tissue paper (plain, acid-free, or non-tarnishing) or clean newsprint is fine for most crafts. Avoid colored tissue or used newspapers; they can bleed or stain. Bag jewelry and fabric crafts in plastic. Seal the jewelry, but leave the fabric packages open to prevent mildew.

Extra fragile items, such as glass, fine metal sculpture, or ceramics, need covering and sealing in special wraps. Materials such as kimpak or bubble wrap can be purchased through local packing suppliers listed in your yellow pages. In fact, both Sears and Montgomery Ward have a general selection of good packing materials. Use the cushioned coverings generously and seal all edges to make a small, secure package of breakables.

The pieces are now ready for boxing. Local suppliers will sell you exact-sized cartons, but you can save money if you collect used ones from neighborhood stores. Grocery and liquor stores dispose of sturdy cartons, but if you want the top-of-the-line in used materials, check out a bookstore. Their cartons come in various sizes and are especially durable.

Before placing the craft in the box, pad the bottom. Shredded newsprint, old newspapers, tissue paper, or any of the more expensive materials, such as shredded foam, polystyrene flakes, kimpak, or bubble wrap will cushion your work from rough handling or bumpy roads. Some inventive crafters have used wood chips, popcorn, or corn husks. Whatever is used should surround the objects by several inches on top, bottom, and sides. This puts the craft securely in the middle and protects it from the Mack truck that will undoubtedly be placed on top of it at the post office. Right on top put a packing slip that identifies the contents, unpacking and repacking instructions (for returns), and a new catalog and order blank. Close the box. Seal it with gummed tape or nylon filament tape. The outside of the package, just like a letter, requires receiver's address, return address, and correct postage. THIS

SIDE UP, HANDLE WITH CARE, and FRAGILE labels should be visible. They don't guarantee anything, but at least you and the buyer know you tried.

It isn't a bad idea to wrap an imaginary order. Have UPS or the post office check it out to see if it meets their specifications. You can even send it to yourself or a friend to see how well your package survives shipping. Better to make corrections now than to lose orders later.

If you have special concerns, consult *The Modern Packaging Encyclopedia* (McGraw-Hill, Inc., 1221 Avenue of the Americas, New York, NY 10091) or *Packing and Shipping of Crafts* (American Craft Council, 44 West 53rd Street, New York, NY 10091). These sources cover the subject in great detail.

Your responsibility in packaging stops with the shipper. From drop-off to delivery, it's up to him. You'll want to deal with an outfit that offers quick transit, prompt delivery, adequate insurance coverage, careful handling, and low cost. No one service is the best in all situations.

The US Post Office is handiest to most people. Despite its poor reputation, you'll get pretty good rates, handling, and delivery service. If you're sending out small packages in limited quantity, start here. You can use either first- or fourth-class mail. First-class mail is costly, currently $.13 for the first ounce, $.11 per ounce for the second through thirteenth ounce, and a flat $1.56 for a fourteen- through sixteen-ounce package. Rates over a pound depend on the customer's postal zone as well as weight. For your money you can send as much as seventy pounds in a package up to one hundred inches long and around combined. (The post office calls this length plus girth.). For $1.20 you can insure it for up to $200. If you want additional insurance, you can register the package to get unlimited coverage. Rates for registering go by weight, with a minimum of $2.10. Packages under thirteen ounces usually travel by air; heavier ones go by "the fastest transportation available."

Fourth-class mail, or parcel post, is cheaper. Between large cities, or "first-class post offices," you can send as much as forty pounds in a container up to eighty-four inches long and around combined. Smaller post offices, for some reason, can accept larger packages. The rate schedule is determined by distance and weight. Parcel post cannot be registered, so the maximum insurance coverage you can obtain is $200. Fourth-class is O.K. if you're not in a hurry and the delivery point isn't too distant. For most craftspeople, parcel post is adequate anytime except holidays.

Other services offered by the post office are COD delivery, special delivery, special handling, and express mail. The post office will collect on COD orders up to $300 for a small fee, usually a dollar or two, including insurance protection. You must still pay the postage, but if you include the cost of shipping in the bill to your customer, you'll be reimbursed for this expense.

Special delivery service gets your package to the customer's door as soon as possible after it arrives at the post office, even on Sundays and holidays. The cost runs a dollar or two in addition to postage, but could be a lifesaver if you're late shipping an order. A second cousin to special delivery, special handling is available for parcel post. It provides quicker than normal delivery at reasonable cost (a maximum of $1, plus postage, for a package over ten pounds).

If you're in a real rush to get your package to a customer, and you both happen to live near large cities, you can do even better than special delivery by sending it by express mail. The price is steep, but the post office guarantees next-day delivery. Rates vary by weight and zone, but the minimum charge is $7.50 delivered to the customer, $5.40 if he is willing to pick it up at his post office.

Whether you use first-class, fourth-class, or special delivery, the post office has printouts that explain packaging requirements, shipping costs, and insurance rates that will help you assess their services.

Uncle Sam's biggest competitor for package delivery is United Parcel Service (UPS). It is equal to or surpasses the US Post Office in almost every respect. For one thing, the rates, based on weight, distance, and mode of transit (ground or air), are usually cheaper than postal rates. Insurance is cheaper, too. The first $100 are insured free, and for a quarter you can buy an additional $100 worth of coverage. There is a maximum coverage, however, of $5000 for ground transit and $1000 for air. Because every package is signed for, tracing lost ones is simple. In fact, UPS claims only a 2 percent damage or loss rate. Ninety-eight-percent perfect deliveries takes much of the gamble out of shipping fragile crafts works.

Best of all, delivery is fast. Local deliveries are made within a day, and longer distances are covered in two to five days.

An added bonus is the UPS pick-up service. Instead of taking your packages to a depot, you can arrange to have them picked up at your home or place of business. Some craftspeople schedule regular pickups, such as once a week. The charge is $2 to $4 (depending on where you live), no matter how many packages you have, so it pays to send as many at one time as possible. You are limited, however, to one hundred pounds per day to any one receiver. With pickups, weighing is your responsibility, so make sure you have an accurate scale. If you put insufficient postage on your packages, they'll come back to you. And that's no bargain.

UPS accepts packages up to fifty pounds and 108 inches, length and girth combined. Like the post office, it will deliver COD orders. The main limitation of UPS is that it does not deliver out of the United States.

The chart below will help you compare at a glance size and insurance limitations of the three most common methods of shipping crafts works, so that you can see which best suits your needs.

PER PACKAGE MAXIMUMS FOR MOST COMMON SHIPPING METHODS

	Weight	*Dimensions* Length + Girth	*Insurance* *Coverage*
First-Class	70 lb.	100 inches	no limit
Fourth-Class	40 lb.	84 inches	$200
UPS	50 lb.	108 inches	$1000 air $5000 ground

The post office and UPS aren't the only ways to go. Furniture makers, big-time sculptors, and other craftspeople whose work exceeds weight and size limitations can make use of the bus lines, air freight, air freight forwarders, or common carriers to solve their shipping problems. Although rates may vary, the bus lines travel as quickly, in most cases, as UPS. The receiver, however, must arrange to pick up the item at the bus station. Just as the bus lines deliver from depot to depot, air freight shippers go from airport to airport. Both systems are inconvenient to customers. Air freight forwarders, on the other hand, will deliver to the customer's door. The cost is high, but the service is excellent. Insurance cannot exceed $500, but there's no limit on dimensions. They'll even ship and deliver around the world.

The final choice is a common carrier. It is last for good reason. The rates are based on a five-hundred-pound minimum, and insurance goes for about $.60 a pound. Interstate trucking services or moving companies are common carriers that will handle over-sized crafts works if you need their services. It isn't cheap, and it is slow. Consider it only as a last resort.

To be successful in mail order you must be more than a talented, high-quality craftsperson. You must be an ad designer, a photographer, writer, researcher, cataloger, packager, mailer, and possibly kit maker. You must be acquainted with federal, state, and local regulations, as well as taxes, licenses, and zoning statutes. Mail order isn't for a person who has no stomach for business. There's simply too much of it to swallow. But if you want to stay at home with your craft, take the time to do the homework and develop the skills needed to make direct mail sales work for you.

CHAPTER EIGHT

Augmenting Your Crafts Income

When sales are slow and you feel a need to moonlight, or even when times are good but you like the idea of earning extra dollars, why not try a craft-related sideline? That way, you'll keep old friends, make new contacts, and possibly learn more about your trade.

You can choose a job that nets a nice profit but still leaves time and energy to work at your bench. Seem impossible? Then you probably haven't thought about teaching, lecturing, or any number of other activities that do just that.

Many of these avocations generate other money-making opportunities. As a shop owner, for instance, you can peddle the wares of others or rent out space for classes. If you decide to write, you can easily recycle your articles into books or kits. But no matter what sideline you pick, you can use it to promote your craft. The publicity you receive will not only spur the sale of your goods, but will also allow you to charge— and get—more for your handwork.

For many of these ventures, little experience is needed to get launched. For example, if you've ever demonstrated your craft at a fair or answered questions about one of your techniques, you were teaching, whether you knew it or not.

What remains is to learn how to get paid for what you've been giving away all along.

As a beginner, you are most likely to be hired by groups that cater to hobbyists or novices. These include adult ed programs, the YW–YMCA, neighborhood and civic centers, parks and recreation departments, and scouting organizations. Sometimes prisons, army bases, hospitals, and nursery schools also have a need for crafts instructors. You can locate most of these groups in the yellow pages of your phone directory.

When applying for a position, submit a written description of your class to the director along with a sample project. As you draw up this presentation, keep in mind that most people learn crafts best by doing them. That means each session should open with a demonstration on one, possibly two, new techniques. The remainder of the time should be used for students to apply what they've learned, while you encourage, advise, and assist them.

Even though the lessons themselves will be simple, try to include as many details in your plan as possible. Tell the director how many weeks the course will run, how many hours per lesson, and what skills the students will gain. Since most classes have a minimum enrollment, promote yours among your friends to ensure it won't be cancelled. Once you are established you won't need to do this. Your former students will pass the word.

In competition with educational and civic groups are crafts supply stores and other commercial enterprises. They often promote the sale of materials by sponsoring free classes in everything from macrame to rug hooking. Here again, expertise counts more than teaching ability. In fact, large companies, like Lee Wards, specially train their instructors and keep them up to date with frequent seminars. Since the competition is keen for these jobs, your best chance of being hired is if you have something extra to offer. This could be a new technique, superior ability, or an established reputation. No matter what makes you special, be sure to emphasize it.

As you search for commerial teaching opportunities, remember that any business that stocks crafts materials could use your services. Some examples are paint and wallpaper stores, florists, and hobby centers. If you can't find stores near you that sponsor crafts instruction, don't be put off. Mary Thimme created her own teaching job by convincing a florist to let her hold classes in his back room. Because she offered to work on commission, he had nothing to lose. Before long, her reputation grew and along with it her wages.

Of course, there is no reason you can't set up your own private classes. Many craftspeople like teaching out of their homes because expenses are low and they keep most of the money they bring in. Others give lessons to help subsidize a studio, small store, or production facility.

Wherever you do the instructing, certain questions have to be answered. Do you want to teach individuals or groups? Should you charge a flat fee or an hourly rate? What should the amount be? Since the going rate differs from place to place, you'll have to do some investigating to determine what amounts are appropriate in your locality.

You also should have a special spot, like a basement or back room, used just for teaching. To discourage hangers-on, set a definite quitting time and stick to it. One potter used to punctuate the end of his classes by having his wife pick him up promptly at the end of each one.

Advertising is a must, too. Although word-of-mouth is best,

you might also consider a classified ad in the local newspaper, a listing in the yellow pages, or a poster on the community bulletin board.

Apprenticeships are a form of private classes for crafts such as pottery and jewelry-making that require in-depth training. Of course, to be a master teacher, you must be very advanced in your craft and have built up a reputation. If and when you meet these qualifications, there are several ways to run an apprenticeship program. Some are structured like college courses. Students pay by the quarter, and time each day is set aside for formal instruction. Other masters operate more casually. Teaching is done on a one-to-one basis, there is no set curriculum, and tuition is so much per class session, payable if and when the student attends.

Occasionally the master doesn't charge tuition; he profits by getting considerable labor for a low wage. One successful weaver in the Midwest admits he couldn't operate his designing business without his paid apprentices. He often contracts with mass producers to create a number of designs in a short time. To work up thirty-five pillow samples within a month would be impossible for him alone, so his assistants are really extensions of himself. However, they don't mind because they have some leeway in executing the designs and are happy to be paid for doing something they enjoy. Learning from one of the best weavers is, of course, the main employee benefit.

Because there are so few apprenticeships in the United States, the National Endowment for the Arts has established a Master Craftsworker Apprenticeship Program. One of its functions is to give out twenty grants annually. Of each $3,000 stipend, the master receives $300 and the student the rest.

Perhaps this project will encourage more advanced craftspeople to take on apprentices. Right now that is the only way they can teach without a degree. While post secondary vocational schools are allowed to hire instructors without this credential, they rarely do. At the college level, requirements are even stiffer. A part-time instructor needs a Masters of Fine Arts to teach undergraduate art majors; associate and full professors need doctorates.

Even so, as interest in crafts grows, more and more colleges and universities are expanding their arts programs. As a result, they need additional teachers. Therefore, higher education is a fertile job field for any serious artisan who is willing to get the extra schooling.

Contemporary Crafts Marketplace (R. R. Bowker Co., 1180 Avenue of the Americas, New York, NY 10036) lists institutions that offer courses in crafts. They include universities, colleges, private workshops, museum schools, and art centers. The entries are arranged alphabetically by state and give school addresses, type of craft instruction, and degrees granted.

Another good source is *By Hand: A Guide to Schools and a Career in Crafts* (E.P. Dutton, 201 Park Avenue South, New York, NY 10003). This book lists college courses, arts centers, workshops, crafts cooperatives, and apprenticeship programs. For major entries, the authors evaluate the levels of instruction and their appropriateness for beginners or advanced students. *By Hand* is a valuable tool for locating training to enable you to teach or for finding possible employers, should you already have the credentials.

A degree can open the door to other specialties in the field of art education besides teaching. One is art therapy. The art therapist typically works with emotionally disturbed or physically handicapped patients on an individual basis. Art activities are used as a vehicle for expression, therapy, and diagnosis. For example, an emotionally disturbed child might be taught to finger paint. Not only would this be a constructive activity for the child, but it would provide the therapist with clues to the child's emotional state. Once trained, a therapist can work in mental institutions, hospitals, guidance centers, or schools.

Another teaching-related field would be setting up and running an education program for an art museum. Such a program might include a degreed program for serious art students, after-school classes in arts and crafts for children, lectures about the museum's exhibits, demonstrations of art techniques, television programs about the museum or local art activities, and guided tours of the facilities. Museums often hire librarians with a specialty in art history and materials for this job, but such trained people are hard to find. A solid crafts and art history background could land you such a position.

Teaching, however, can be an all-consuming job. For many craftspeople it robs too much time from the bench. If something less time-consuming, yet no less lucrative is what you're after, then you might consider lecturing. Anyone who has taught or has had some success communicating ideas to apprentices is capable of earning money lecturing. Social fraternities, luncheon clubs, church auxiliary organizations, and community centers all need speakers for their frequent meetings. These groups consume subjects at a phenomenal pace, and your special approach to crafts may be just what is needed to liven up a politically heavy schedule. A fabric craftswoman I know takes advantage of the contrast of crafts to business. She lectures at business conventions. While the men are busy with their meetings, she entertains their wives with talk about macrame or new crafts ideas.

You may be thinking that you could never get up in front of all those people. Just remember that the lectern is forbidding to most people at first. Even experienced teachers have a tough time making the transition from classroom to meeting hall. But experience will give you the poise you need.

The best way to think of a local speaking engagement is that it's like a casual chat. If you tell the audience at the outset you're not a public speaker, you will enlist their understanding and support. You can also invite audience participation. Have them ask questions so the talk can be even more conversational. Don't strive for a highly structured presentation of facts. You'll end up reading to the audience rather than talking to them, and no one likes that. Have an outline—main points you don't want to miss—then just talk. A few humorous lines to punctuate your points will help relax you and the audience. There are a number of encyclopedias of humor at your library. You can look up specific subjects to get a good line or two. Or you might subscribe to a humor service which supplies fresh and timely lines weekly or monthly. The best of these is Robert Orben's *Current Comedy* (801 Wilmington Trust Bldg., Wilmington, DE 19801). As you gain experience, you'll get the hang of delivering clever lines.

Having what educators call "visual aids" will also liven up your presentation. Arrange to include slides, photos, or crafts products themselves. A small demonstration of a technique will stimulate interest and probably put you at ease as well.

Begin with a friendly audience. The church, club, or social organization you belong to is apt to be supportive of your first efforts. Crafts guilds, associations, or companies that relate to your craft could be next. Your library has several encyclopedias of associations that list these organizations. If you don't mind traveling, you can offer to present workshops at state or regional chapters. The groups will arrange for your transportation and accommodations and pay you a sum for speaking. Once you have established a reputation, they will come to you.

As you gain experience and confidence, you might want to expand your act to take in a national lecture circuit. There are lecture bureaus in most major cities which arrange speaking tours. But for this you should be a bit of a ham, because at this level, it's show business.

Although some people enjoy lecturing, others are more comfortable putting their thoughts down on paper. If that describes you, and you have something to tell others that is new or unique, maybe you should consider writing.

Breaking into print, however, isn't easy. The general magazines that pay well, such as *Family Circle* and *Better Homes and Gardens,* have stiff requirements and use only a few crafts stories per issue. The more specialized publications, like *Lapidary Journal* and *Make it with Leather,* buy more handcraft pieces, but they pay little or nothing. But don't dismiss the obscure or low-paying publications at first. They offer you a place to establish yourself as a professional crafts writer. After that, sales to the better publications will be easier. Community newspapers often buy articles written by a beginning journalist, especially one who is an expert in his or her field. Such sales won't make you rich, but you'll accumulate a pile of articles in print which can be mentioned the next time you try to sell an article.

To find buyers for your article ideas, consult *Writer's Market* (an annual publication of *Writer's Digest Magazine,* 9933 Alliance Road, Cincinnati, OH 45242). It lists most of the publishers of magazines, books, and newspapers in the

United States and Canada, giving rates, how and when you'll be paid, word length, type of articles, photo requirements, and a whole lot more. And one section of *Contemporary Crafts Marketplace* (American Crafts Council, R.R. Bowker Co., 1180 Avenue of the Americas, New York, NY 10036) gives an alphabetical listing of crafts publishers.

Before you send an article to a magazine, send the editor a query letter. This is a letter that outlines briefly what the proposed article will contain. It attempts to hook the editor on your idea by emphasizing its uniqueness and importance. It should also include a list of your credits, such as crafts awards, gallery presentations, your training and background, and other magazines that have published your work. Keep the letter within two pages typed, double spaced. Because this doesn't allow any room for rambling, work hard to give your presentation the greatest punch in the fewest words. The main idea of your article should be contained in the first paragraph of your query letter, and it deserves all of the polish your finished article will receive. In fact, most writers work out the lead for the proposed article in advance to use as the introductory paragraph in the query letter. This is a sensible approach because if an editor isn't impressed by the first sentence or two of a query, chances are he will assume your article will be equally uninspiring and go no further. Give careful attention to the organization, clarity, and cleverness of the rest of the letter, too. Remember, besides selling your idea and qualifications, the query is also selling your writing style.

If the editor likes your idea, he will ask to see the article "on speculation," meaning if he likes it, you'll get paid; if not, he'll send it back. If the article comes back, it doesn't necessarily mean it is no good. It could be that it is similar to something they already had planned or have used recently, or the slant is not appropriate for their magazine. You can avoid some of this discouragement by studying recent issues of the magazine for content and editorial style before you query. If it does come back, send your query to another magazine and try again. Determined writers have been known to make a sale after surviving twenty or more rejects. You'll have to decide how much your article and time are worth. You'll have a greater chance of success if you have more than one article idea out at a time.

Perhaps you'd like to try a full-length book. Just as with an article, send a query first. If the editor is interested in your idea, he'll ask to see a tentative outline and two or three sample chapters. Unlike articles, however, books are seldom done on speculation. If the editor likes your outline and sample chapters, he will offer you a contract to write the book, guaranteeing you a certain sum, usually paid one half in advance and one half on completion of the manuscript. Although you risk more time working up a book presentation than you do with an article, you stand to gain more in the long run, for a good seller may net royalties for years to come.

The importance of querying before investing any real time and effort in writing is illustrated by Mary Kay Davis, author of two books on needlepoint design. Her first book, *Needlepoint from America's Great Quilt Designs,* involved finding historical quilts and translating their patterns into needlework designs. Before any photographs of the designs could be taken, a sample of each had to be worked up. She did all sixty herself so she could anticipate and correct any problems readers might have. "Imagine the time and energy I would have wasted had I done the book first and then couldn't interest an editor in it," she says.

If you have a great idea for a book and think others could benefit from what you have to share, but you feel your writing skills are not what they should be, there is no reason why you can't seek out an established author who is willing to collaborate and share the profits. After all, when two professionals work together, their product usually is better than either could have done alone. Sometimes craftspeople who are interested in increased sales from the publicity fallout subsidize a writer/photographer.

Don't worry unnecessarily if you lack photographic or graphic design skills either. Crafts photography and illustration are such highly technical arts that most publishers insist on the right to use a professional of their choosing to do the job.

Free-lancing isn't the only means of earning money with your writing. The federal government hires craftspeople with administrative, research, and writing skills. Most of them work for the Department of Agriculture, the Smithsonian Institution, the Bureau of Indian Affairs, the National Endowment for the Arts, and the Armed Forces. State and local governments also have a need for crafts writers, as do crafts associations and trade publications.

One form of writing often leads to another. Mary Kay Davis now writes a column for a small newspaper; it is soon to be syndicated. She also does kit designing for magazines, such as *Better Homes and Gardens*. For her, that is more profitable and easier than trying to package and market them herself. "You would end up with a product that couldn't compete with mass-produced items in price or quality," Mary Kay says.

Manufacturers also buy kit designs. If you would like to try your hand at this, study the numerous ones available in department, hobby, and even toy stores. Think up similar short projects a hobbyist could make without any trouble.

Then write to the manufacturer. (Get his address from the boxes his other products come in.) Send just enough details to stimulate his interest. If he asks to see a sample, deliver it in person or send it by registered mail. This is precaution against plagiarism, necessary for the few companies who aren't reputable. To ensure return of your product, enclose postage or authorize them to mail it collect.

Mass producers also need designs for their products. Ceramists, glassblowers, and silversmiths are a few of the craftspeople who either work for one company or free-lance for several. Each of these designers considers the needs of everyone making or using the product. He then creates a design that suits the most needs.

If you think you would like to be an in-house designer, you can locate possible employers by consulting *Thomas' Register of Manufacturers,* available in most libraries. This directory lists more than eighty-five thousand companies by the type of product they make. Since chief executives are also listed, it's a useful tool should you decide to free-lance. In that case, you would simply write to one of them explaining your idea, exactly as you would to sell a kit design. Another handy guide for free-lancers is *Artists and Photographer's Market* (another annual publication of *Writer's Digest Magazine).* It lists opportunities in the fashion, toy, needlework, textile, and metal industries.

In many larger firms, designers have assistants who construct their plans in three dimensions. Model makers make these samples out of clay, while sample makers fabricate the real thing. One of these may be just the job if you want to stay working with your hands.

On a smaller scale, cottage industries need craftspeople who don't mind reproducing the same item again and again or repeating one step continuously, assembly-line fashion. You needn't go to Appalachia to find such jobs. Small crafts-production operations exist in towns and cities all over the country. Susan Ushman runs such a business in Chicago, selling fabric purses through the party plan, much like Tupperware markets its plastic-ware.

Susan's operation is much simpler than Tupperware's, however, because she has only one product; all the bags are cut from the same pattern. No two are identical, however, because each is made of a different fabric. She is able to keep costs down because so little material is needed for each bag that they can be made from inexpensive designer samples.

At each party customers decide which swatches they like best. The swatches are then sent to several local housewives who are skilled seamstresses to be made into purses. These workers are paid by the piece, and the hostess receives a free bag for her effort.

You can track down such cottage industries in your community through local crafts associations. Also, *The Contemporary Crafts Marketplace* lists many of them alphabetically by state.

As a moonlighter you don't have to sell just your know-how and expertise—you can sell your goods retail as well. By eliminating the middleman, you'll make more money, receive payment immediately, and get valuable feedback from the customers about what they'd like to buy. And it's as easy as staging a boutique-style garage sale.

Actually, this event is held in your home. Like any other retail operation, its success depends on its ability to attract customers. Advertising is essential. And the most effective means is word-of-mouth. Tell all your friends and have them tell their friends. Send out personal invitations to everyone you can think of who might be interested. And follow the example of teachers advertising private classes and place an ad in the paper or put up posters in neighborhood stores. If you have your customers sign a guest book, you can add their names to your mailing list for future sales.

Offering a variety of wares in a wide price range will attract a better turnout, so unless you are an expert in many crafts and prolific as well, you'll benefit from inviting other artisans to show their merchandise too. Just be sure your goods get top billing. To keep track of consignments, use a color-coded tag on each item. When it is purchased, remove the tag and store it in a drawer until you are ready to do the accounting.

Don't worry about having enough space. When you are forced to use every square inch of your home, you'll find your ingenuity working overtime to create a place for everything. Two other bits of advice from those experienced in these events—have a sizeable amount of money on hand for change, and don't accept personal checks unless you know the patron well.

Another way to get a taste of retailing is to rent space in a public market, just as farmers do to sell their produce. For a few dollars per day and a small percentage of the gross, you're in business. In this case, advertising isn't so important because the other merchants will create a certain amount of traffic that you can trade off of. You should, however, do something to attract attention on the spot. Usually the easiest means is to demonstrate your craft, which also allows you to work and sell at the same time. In many areas of the country indoor flea markets are also popular. The buildings which house them are divided into booths which are rented on a short-term basis.

Another variation is the shopping mall bazaar usually held at holiday times.

If you work in your own studio, you might consider creating a display nook somewhere on the premises. This is an easy and inexpensive way to sell your merchandise at a good profit. Tourists and bargain hunters are always seeking out factory showrooms, common in the pottery and glassware fields, to save money on seconds, test items, and discontinued wares. Even if your products are sold at half the retail price, you still earn at least the wholesale amount, while the customer gets a bargain.

If, like quilts or wall-sized rugs, your products are expensive to make and can't be sold at wholesale prices to make a profit, your home might be the best place to sell them. However, unless you live in a commercial district, you'll have to put a lot of effort into promotion. Paid advertising or extra services, such as teaching or selling supplies, may draw interested customers. If they're satisfied, word will spread. Soon your reputation may be your best advertisement.

If opening a retail store, selling others' work as well as your own, is your ambition, it is a good idea to spend some time working in someone else's store before plunging into your own. Not only is there no risk, but you'll be getting paid for your on-the-job schooling. The procedures will be introduced one step at a time, and you'll get practice at all the jobs related to owning a shop.

Let the owner know the kinds of experience you're after. Offer to help with the bookkeeping. Then familiarize yourself with other phases of his operation. This should include handling peak business hours, preparing displays, taking inventory, making change, sweeping the front walk, and making friends with the guy next door. Even if you don't know what questions to ask, the typical crafts store owner is willing to guide the enthusiastic beginner in the ways of running a store.

New Englander Adam Jackson has hired and trained several craftspeople who later opened their own shops. He says, "I like what I'm doing, and I kind of like to help out the new kid on the block. Maybe I've just been lucky, but the folks I've hired who later start their own places are just about the hardest workers I know. On top of that, they're good company. Our interests are the same. My success is their success, so we both make out real well in the end."

Working alongside a veteran will show you two things. It will give you a clear idea of the complexities of retailing, and it will let you know if this is the move for you.

If you haven't had any retailing experience, a little soul-searching is in order to see if you're a business manager type. Running a store requires a great deal of time and energy and will likely leave little time for your own craft. Do you like people? Are you well organized? Do you like responsibility? making decisions? Are you willing to work long hours? have few holidays? Do you stick to a goal in the face of discouragement? If you can answer yes to most of these questions, owning a store may be for you.

Your first consideration will be money. You're going to need a lot of it. Count on having a year's financing to tide you over until the profits begin rolling in. To estimate how much you will need, prepare a budget that plans for advertising, insurance, legal and professional fees, utilities, office and store supplies, taxes and licenses, rent, merchandise, equipment, and miscellaneous expenses. And don't forget to include a salary for yourself and any employees you may need.

Anticipate and prepare for financial emergencies. No doubt Christmas will be the peak selling season. If you hope to draw a lot of tourists, the summer month could run a close second. But you'll need reserves to see you through the seasonal slumps. It is important to raise enough cash before you begin. The Small Business Administration names inadequate financing as one of the principal causes of business failures.

If you already have enough in your personal savings to cover anticipated expenses, you're all set. If not, go to friends, relatives, or other people who might be willing to back your venture. Be careful, however, that enough of the money invested is your own to assure your control of the operation. Supplies and equipment companies will probably sell you what you need on credit. You can buy it now, pay for it later when your business has begun to make a profit. After you've logged some experience with your new business and carefully worked out your financial status and requirements, you may be able to obtain additional cash from a bank or other lending institution.

Some craftspeople solve their financing problems by going in with a partner. This could be doubly helpful if you can find someone with skills, time, or knowledge that you lack. Others bridge money gaps by sharing a space with someone else.

Another major concern when opening a store is finding a good location. Do a good deal of scouting before you settle on a place. You need to be sure the community needs a crafts shop. Find out about the makeup of the community in which you hope to open. Are the people of the age, occupation, and income who would be apt to buy what you have to sell? Is the character of the neighborhood changing, from residential to industrial, rural to suburban, for example?

Are there a number of competitive businesses already in the area? The US Census Bureau publishes a list of kinds of businesses and the number of people living in an area necessary to support each type of business. For example, it gives the number of inhabitants necessary to support a gift shop at 12,386. Thus, a typical town with a population of 24,000 could theoretically support two gift shops. If there are already three gift shops in that town, it might not be wise, then, to open another, unless it happens to be a tourist center, or have some other reason that there might be a need for one.

If you have a particular store in mind, check the history of the particular site you are considering. If the building has been vacant for a long time or there has been a high turnover of businesses occupying the building, it could be that it is an unprofitable location. Also check zoning ordinances, parking availability, accessibility to public transportation, and surrounding businesses.

Shopping centers are great locations, but rents are high. If you can find a gathering place for craftspeople in your community, this would be ideal. In Louisville, Kentucky, for example, a number of small establishments, from a Christmas boutique to a handmade-pillow shop, are nestled together in a converted three-story bakery, appropriately called Bakery Square. In Chicago the Old Town area draws local artisans. See if you can find a crafts colony in your town.

Sources to check to find answers to questions about the suitability of a location are the US Census Bureau, your chamber of commerce, state development agencies, crafts associations, local real estate companies, local newspapers, banks, and city offices.

Rather than starting your store from scratch, you may decide to buy a going business. Again, a lot of care needs to go into your decision. If the store is in a good location, has usable fixtures, the previous owner had a good reputation, and the price is right, this may be a wise investment, because you save the time of equipping and stocking the store, and you ll have a ready-made clientele. You might also be able to benefit from the previous owner's experience.

Once you start your retail business, keep an eye on your inventory. Make sure you're stocking what people will buy. And plan to add some extra features that will help draw in customers, such as sponsoring shows, classes, or free demonstrations, selling hobby supplies, or even working in your display window.

For additional information on starting your store, enlist the help of the Small Business Administration. They publish a number of booklets on all aspects of starting and running a small business. (Write to Superintendent of Documents, US Government Printing Office, Washington, DC 20402, for their publications list.) They also offer loans and free or low-cost technical advice and assistance.

Once you are established as an entrepreneur, new doors will open into wholesaling or several other retailing careers. But that's the way it is with sidelines—one begets another. Writers become syndicated, designers open their own schools, street peddlers turn into sales agents. At some point, there's a risk that your new endeavors may not leave time for your handcrafting. To guard against this, start any new venture in a small way and expand slowly, if at all.

On the other hand, you may get hooked on your side activity and decide you'd rather be a teacher, seller, designer, or writer than a candlestick maker. Fine! The craft world is broad enough to encompass any number of skills beyond your bench. Art can be as rewarding in the appreciation as in the doing.

CHAPTER NINE

Selling Yourself

A craftsperson without publicity is like a man winking at a girl in the dark. He knows what he's doing, but no one else does.

If you want to sell your crafts, you can't afford to be shy or modest. You'll have to be sure other people know what you're doing and why it is special. Or no sales. Many artists feel uncomfortable as salesmen, but it's really not so hard as you might think. If you're enthusiastic about your work, you probably talk about it frequently with friends and relatives. Well, the conversation you have with a buyer or the editor of a newspaper is no different. You are still talking to one person at a time about what you know best—your craft. The difference is he or she can tell a lot of other people about it. If you find it extremely difficult to promote your work, you can let others handle publicity by selling through co-ops, shops, and fairs, but you still have to do a little public relations to get into these.

A good place to start is with some free publicity. Since you probably have a limited budget, you'll want to aim for the most exposure for the least money. Paid advertising can always come later. Besides, it's more suspect than someone else's promoting your work in a newspaper story. How can you get this free publicity? By telling an editor about yourself. That's how most of the stories about crafts get written. Editors have a lot of space to fill and appreciate hearing about newsworthy items.

But there is one major rule to remember. You have to find something unique about your work or yourself, because thousands of others in your state probably do the same craft. Is there something special about the kind of objects you make, or the materials you use? If your work isn't different, maybe you are. A psychiatrist who makes necklaces will attract interest, even if his necklaces don't. Perhaps how you got started is noteworthy, or how you keep going. If someone has ever said to you, "How unusual," there's your angle, and you'll use it over and over again to make people remember you.

The local media are hungry for material about unusual residents. Recently I read a news story about someone who makes doilies out of human hair, a revival of an early American craft. Another feature was about a potter who is blind. "Understand that newspapers are interested in things that are new and different," said John Oppendahl, city editor of the *Detroit News*. Take your unusual angle to the major newspapers, radio, and television. Even if you are just appearing at an art fair, or speaking before a women's group, contact the smaller community papers. You may not get a full page, but at the very least, you'll get some notice for your event.

Before you can take advantage of this free publicity, you'll have to do some ground work. Start out by making a list of all the newspapers in your area—dailies, weeklies, newsletters, and the local television and radio stations. Follow them closely for several weeks, noting any stories about crafts. As you make your list, indicate where each item appeared, so you'll know where to send your piece. A feature story on the news pages should go to the city editor, but something about earrings or other items for women should go to the women's editor. Gallery openings or art shows are directed to the art editor. Some papers even have separate columns about crafts or shopping information which might mention your work. At radio or television stations, it's the feature editors who decide on the stories. Take the time to find out their names. They get so much mail each day, they are more likely to open an envelope addressed specifically to them.

The standard format for your letter is the press release, and it's not hard to make yours look as professional as those sent by public relations experts. Editors are busy people who get a lot of phone calls, so they prefer to hear about crafts stories by mail. Save them even more time by making your information easy to read. That means typing it on 8½ × 11-inch white paper, using double spacing and one-inch margins all around. Be sure to put your name, address, and telephone number on the top so you can be reached easily if the editor decides to send out a reporter to do your story or if he has to add details you've overlooked.

You need a catchy lead to get an editor's attention. Start off with your unusual angle. "A fourth-generation silversmith is carrying on the family tradition—but she's the first woman to take up the work," would probably keep someone reading, rather than, "I'd like to tell you about my work." In the next few sentences, include all the important information: who, what, when, where, and why, the journalist's five W's. If you don't have an angle, find something else to stress. The event may be important: "The annual Ann Arbor Art Fair, featuring artists from all over the Midwest, will be held on

July 21st from 10 AM to 9 PM on State Street." Or the place: "The Civic Center Gardens will provide a scenic backdrop for Mary Sharp's sculpture exhibit next Thursday." Perhaps the person is noteworthy: "Meredith Jacobs, the mayor's daughter, will be the only area weaver to be included in the Art Institute's state show this year."

Try to get as much exposure as possible from your release. Send it to all the media outlets on your list. But if you are aiming for a feature story, send it to only one place at a time, giving each a few days to respond before giving them a follow-up call. Editors don't want to see a story they're running appear in several papers at the same time. You can assure an editor in your letter that you've come to his or her paper first.

If your release gets noticed, you're lucky. But don't be discouraged if it doesn't. You have, after all, made a contact. The editor might keep it on file for future use. Each time something new happens to you, send out another release. If you're getting into a prestigious show or a well-known store starts selling your work, for example, tell everyone about it. You never know what will catch an editor's fancy.

Timing may make the difference between getting published and remaining anonymous. If you want publicity for a specific event, send in your information two or three weeks ahead, especially to smaller papers that publish only once or twice a week. Even the dailies like having the information early because they often give advance publicity to events which they don't cover in depth. Magazines work two to six months ahead.

Radio and television programs are also interested in local craftspeople, but, again, the angle had best be unique. They do fewer features than newspapers, thus must be more selective.

Use the same technique to tell the stations that you'd use on newspapers. Send them a press release. Listen to the programs that interview people or list community events to see where you might fit in. Send your release and photograph directly to the disc jockey or television host, or if you haven't singled him out, to the features editor. Here, too, send to one station at a time for feature stories, waiting a few weeks for a response before trying a rival station. If you can tie in to a community or charitable event like a fund-raising art show, your chances improve.

Publicity becomes promotion when you start spending a little money to tell people about your work. Begin by making your free publicity do double duty. For example, you can "remerchandise" any story about your work and use it as a mailer. Cut out the piece and paste it on white paper with the date and name of the publication on the top. Take it to a quick print shop and have inexpensive copies made. After you send one to all your relatives and old art teachers, mail a copy to every past and possible business contact: show promoters, local galleries, crafts or museum shops, suppliers, and customers. You'll get lots of exposure for precious little effort.

Photographs are vital for your self-promotion campaigns. Whether you are applying to a juried show or sending out a press release, selling through catalogs or presenting a portfolio to a buyer, you'll need them. You can take the pictures yourself if you know a little about photography or you can hire someone to take them. It doesn't have to be expensive. A camera-buff buddy might consider helping you. If you don't know any photo buffs, contact the person in charge of photography at a local high school, community college, or small newspaper. They are often hungry and happy to do some moonlighting. Agree on a single price just for shooting the film, not developing it. It's cheaper for you to have the developing done commercially than for the photographer to charge you per print.

If you have a basic knowledge about photography, you can probably learn how to take your own shots with a little reading and experimenting. You'll need a good 35 mm camera and a tripod. Some lighting equipment is also recommended, but you can shoot outdoors in sunshine if your budget is really tight. The American Crafts Council has put out an excellent book, *Photographing Crafts*, by John C. Barsness. Order it from the American Crafts Council at 44 West 53rd Street, New York, NY 10019. It contains helpful hints on photographic techniques as well as special tips on problems unique to crafts photography, such as showing the texture of pottery or eliminating the reflections on jewelry.

You'll need two kinds of pictures. Color slides are most common. They are used when more than one person will be viewing your work, as when you apply to a juried show or make sales presentations. They'll also liven up any lectures you give.

Black and white glossy prints are important, too. You'll use them for portfolios, catalog sales, and press releases. Even if newspapers don't use them, the photographs may convince an indifferent editor to feature your product. Community newspapers have more limited resources than the dailies and are usually happy to print any good stills. They want high quality black-and-white 8 × 10 glossies. Be sure your name, address, and telephone number are on the back or pasted to a piece of paper below the photo. Don't use a pen to write on a print's backside. Too often the impression shows through.

Remember that your purpose is to get the best shot of your craft object, not to create a fancy picture. A simple background that doesn't compete with your product works best. For black-and-white prints, choose neutral colored backgrounds (white, grey, or black). When using color slides, make sure the background harmonizes with the object but remains secondary. There should be no obvious textures or designs behind the piece, and that includes the overly-common drapery effects. Don't include more than one object in the picture, unless you're trying to show relative size or more than one side of the same piece. A necklace lying on a jewelry box or a chair next to a wall hanging can give a viewer important information. Experiment with different angles and lighting techniques, but always get as close as you can to the object. If you're too far away, much of the detail will be lost.

Publicity releases demand a more interesting shot, something with human interest. For these, show yourself working in your studio or displaying your crafts at an exhibit. An alive photograph is as important as a unique press release. Even if you are highlighting the object itself, you should make the background more interesting. This time put the necklace on a pretty neck or the glass sculpture on a table. This means two sets of photos—human interest prints for the news media and product pictures for everyone else. That's more work, but publicity is work that pays dividends.

When mailing photographs, take care to protect your investment. Use envelopes big enough so the prints don't have to be folded, and insert a piece of stiff cardboard. "Do not bend" written on the envelope will help prevent damage. Color slides can be protected by wrapping them first and mailing in padded envelopes (which you can buy at most stationery stores). Write "hand cancel" on these so the machines at the post office won't brutalize them. A final tip: write the address on the envelope *before* you put in the pictures, or the pen impression may ruin your prints.

Some experts say the promotional item which is cheapest and easiest to distribute is the business card. "If you want to be a professional, you have to act like one," a printer told me. Some of his customers have their cards made before they even begin their business. For a minimal cost of about $25 a thousand, you'll find your investment repaid many times. Even if you restrict your sales to art shows, the cards are useful. A stained glass designer said that he invested in business cards because he was getting a sore arm writing his name and address at art shows. Because he does a lot of custom designs, the cards were an important link to people who would call him later for special orders.

Everyone finds his own special uses for the cards. One glassblower I know uses an oversized business card so she has room to describe her unusual technique and suggest various uses for the object she makes. A jewelry maker I once bought a necklace from wrote a story about the beads on the back of her card to personalize the sale. Most show promoters don't object to your displaying the cards in your exhibit, so even those no-purchase browsers can pick one up. Or you can staple a card to each purchaser's bag. Whatever way you decide to use them, the cards are a professional way for you to introduce yourself.

To make the greatest impression, aim for a unique card. Perhaps that unusual angle from your press release might be modified. A symbol or logo which reflects your work would be valuable. You may even want to do your own lettering and have a printer just make copies. Silkscreen artists, for example, could do their own designs to show off their technique. Even if a professional printer is doing all your work, you can make a distinctive statement by choosing a different typeface or with paper and ink colors. Don't feel obliged to use a white card printed with black ink. The kind of card you create is limited only by your imagination and budget. Just remember to include your name, address, telephone number (with area code), and the name of your craft.

The same design on your business card can be used for other promotional products which create an identity that people will associate with your work. When you are not around to present your business card, labels or tags on your work can be your silent salesmen. They need to be informative and attractive. If you sell through stores, a label is an important way to tell salesclerks and customers about your product. It might describe your method, or the fabric or material you use. Perhaps the place of production is the significant feature. Because the label will be small, choose the phrasing that will most impress a customer.

When a person buys your product, the label goes home too. The advertising continues to work for you months and years beyond the initial sale. If the customer is enthusiastic about your piece, he or she may want to order another one later, or several for gifts. The label should tell the owner where to get it by including either your address or the store's. People also like to be knowledgeable about their purchases. The information on your tag will help them remember your name and some important point about you or your work. As they spread this knowledge to their friends, your label is earning its advertising expense. And label costs are tax-deductible.

Like all promotional items, your labels ought to be unique. Use any kind of materials that are compatible with the product: paper, cardboard, fabric, or wood. Even the way you attach them can vary. Try gluing or sewing them instead of tying. Attractive labels are another way of personalizing your work and distinguishing it from mass-produced items. For this reason, many craftspeople hand make labels instead of having them professionally printed.

The packaging of your piece is still another way to carry out your image. Packaging devices may serve a practical purpose of keeping together items sold in sets or pairs, such as earrings, dishes, coasters, or place mats. But you'll have to be careful to keep the price of the packaging low. Customers may not object to paying a little more if the packaging serves a dual purpose. A pretty ribbon, for example, may hold a set of place mats together, but it can also be used to tie the next present the purchaser has to wrap. A basket to stack coasters in may be a permanent storage piece or could be used as a server. Above all, keep the packaging simple so it doesn't detract from the art itself.

If you are running your own store, packaging for all sales is a must. Your boxes, paper, or bags should have the name and address of your shop, especially when labels are not used on everything. That way, your message will be carried out of the store. With a little imagination, you can keep the price low while building an image for the shop. One owner used linen-textured boxes tied with yarn instead of more expensive and time-consuming gift wrap.

The handbill or flyer can be an effective advertisement for your shop, too. It contains the same essential information as a business card or label, but it can be circulated to large groups of potential buyers. You can mail or distribute flyers to past buyers, area residents, and other potential customers.

When doing the publicity for a fair, the handbills can be placed in high traffic areas to be picked up. You could also place them in crafts stores, libraries, grocery stores, and shopping areas. If your exhibit is at one end of a mall, place the flyers at cashiers throughout the shopping center.

And don't forget the tourist trade. Travellers enjoy buying the work of area artists as reminders of their visit. You could leave flyers in travel agencies, hotels, service stations, auto clubs, and restaurants. One fair promoter even made his flyers into place mats for restaurants.

The cheapest way of producing the flyers is by copying them at the trusty quick print shop. By this inexpensive method, you can get a hundred 8½ × 11 flyers for under $5 and a thousand for about $11. As always, the challenge is to be unique, yet clear, in the layout and presentation. Highlight the most important facts: the who, what, when, where. You'll get the clearest reproduction by using black ink on white paper.

Some craftspeople want to promote specific products. They need brochures which have more information in them than handbills. These are essential if you do a large mail order or wholesale business where the buyer doesn't see the actual object. For more information on designing brochures, refer back to Chapter Seven.

Once you start thinking about promoting your work, you'll be surprised at the other possibilities for free publicity or low-cost advertising. For example, many public institutions display crafts works to make their buildings more interesting and to educate passers-by. Libraries, banks, restaurants, theaters, and hotels or motels are potential places for displays. Any time you spot a crafts display or read about one in any of these buildings, be sure to find out who is in charge and tell him you are available for a display. Make an appointment to bring in some samples of your work. The unique angle comes up again. He may want to know why your work should be featured, so be prepared to explain its uniqueness. You might even suggest a display to a place that has never had one. The key here is to show the management what it can get out of it. A hotel, for instance, might go for the idea as a way of creating more interest in local artists for their travellers. Drop names of other local business people who sponsor displays and endorse the approach.

Giving lectures is another way of exposing your work to potential buyers. Charity groups and women's organizations are always on the look-out for interesting speakers for their meetings. They usually don't have much money for this kind of program, so expect to offer your speech free. Send a press release to a program chairperson or tell people you know who belong to such groups that you would be available. When you go, take samples of your work or colored slides to make your lecture more lively. Always think of who the audience is and emphasize their interests when preparing your lecture. "How to Decorate Your Home with Wall Hangings" could be the title of a weaver's speech to a women's social club. But a speech to museum docents would be more esoteric, such as discussing a new weaving technique.

Teaching, like lecturing, can bring unexpected publicity and sales. This may not be the primary reason you decide to teach a class, but it is a nice side benefit. (See Chapter Eight for more discussion on teaching and lecturing.) You could combine both teaching and lecturing by opening your studio to groups for lecture/demonstrations. Many people would consider this an unusual and educational program for their organization. Some state tourist officials even put out brochures for visitors that list "crafts trails," studios open to the public.

Selling your crafts yourself takes time and effort on a limited budget. You have to take some of your creativity away from making objects to promoting them. Some artists think this is unnecessary—that the work should sell itself. It is true that if your design isn't good, you won't be able to give it away, but too many fine craftspeople remain paupers because they didn't develop a public relations program.

People love crafts because they are unique and personal. Part of the appeal is knowing the person who makes them. When you sell your product, you are also selling yourself.

CHAPTER TEN

The Paperwork

At a dinner party recently I watched, amazed, as the hostess put the final touches on our five-course dinner while dodging her four youngsters, all under five years old, and never seemed to be a bit harried. When I asked how she managed this formidable task, she said, calmly, of course, "It isn't as bad as it seems. They weren't all born at once. I had time to get used to the situation gradually."

If the management details of starting your crafts business seem overwhelming, just remember that procedures, like babies, don't have to be born all at once. In the beginning some very basic knowledge and skills are all that is necessary. As your business grows, so grows the complexity of your procedures. As your business, and income, increases, you will be able to consult professionals to give you the information you need. And, like the hostess, you'll probably handle it with calm efficiency.

Once you have begun to sell your work for profit on a regular basis, you've crossed the line from hobbyist to business operator. Where you go from here is wide open. It can be a backroom sideline or a full-scale corporation. Most craftspeople start small, but a healthy percentage (about 33 percent) get the bug to open their own stores. Big-time or small, you must deal with financial and legal requirements.

Your business name must be registered at the county clerk's office. (It's listed in the phone directory.) Choose whatever name you wish, but don't use "Inc.," "Ltd.," or "Corp." in the name if you're not legally incorporated. You may use the word "Company." There is no need for legal counsel, although you may be charged a registration fee. The registration of your business will enable you to open a commercial account under your assumed name at your bank.

Then write to your state department of taxation or revenue (also listed in the phone book) to request all necessary forms and applications for starting your business. Include the complete name and address of your business, your name and address, the form of business (individual proprietorship, partnership, or corporation), a brief description of your product, and whether you are wholesaling or retailing. There is sometimes a filing fee, but don't worry, they will notify you.

Your state may require a license or permit, and if you're going to be a retailer, there will be state sales taxes to pay and probably local sales and personal property taxes as well.

If you're planning to set up shop in your home, be sure to check the zoning and parking restrictions in your neighborhood. If they say "strictly residential," you may not be able to use your home as a business outlet. A phone call to your town or city municipal offices or the city clerk will clear up this matter.

Begin with the assumption that no matter how small your operation, a certain amount of paperwork will be necessary. You'll have to occasionally write to a customer or supplier, fill out an order, send a bill, and keep records of your income and expenses. The amount will vary with the size and form of your business and what method you use to sell your products, but every businessperson has to file income tax reports and will need some system of recordkeeping.

The time to set up a filing system is before your records get hopelessly out of hand. Disorganized craftspeople have been known to be reduced to tears by a blizzard of misplaced orders, unsold merchandise, uncollected bills, and angry creditors. This shouldn't happen to you if you get organized. Vow never again to throw away a receipt. Keep bank statements, bills, cancelled checks, correspondence, copies of tax returns, and records of income.

Now get two notebooks. Label one "income" and the other "expenses." It should be easy to keep track if you make your entries religiously. Don't overlook any expense which may be deductible on your tax returns. (More on this later.)

More sophisticated bookkeeping systems can be worked out if you take a course or two or tap the knowledge of someone in the field. Look around at your next cocktail party; the guy with the calculator in his pocket is probably an accountant who's anxious to show his stuff. There are also self-teaching systems. Two of the best are the Dome Simplified Weekly Bookkeeping System (Dome Publishing Company, Dome Building, Providence, RI 02903) and the Ideal Simplified Bookkeeping Record (The Ideal System Company, P.O. Box 1568, Augusta, GA 30903).

The simplest system lists income and expenses on a day-to-day basis. If you sold ten wall hangings, twenty plant hangers, and two woven mobiles at your shop today, these sales entries would be listed under income. On the same day if you received an order of wool, bought a new light bulb, and purchased some office supplies, these would be listed as expenses. The difference is the balance. If you keep a running tally, day by day, you'll know if you're ahead or behind.

As business increases, subcategories can be added to your basic lists. Even if you aren't "into" subheadings, they will be necessary if you have to prepare an annual balance sheet. This is a report that lists all your assets and liabilities and is necessary if you want to apply for a business loan.

Assets are all the things you own. They come in four styles—fixed, liquid, tangible, and intangible. Fixed assets include your shop, the land it sits on, kilns, looms, lathes, and other major tools and equipment. Liquid assets are those that can be quickly turned into cash, such as inventory, money people owe you, and money in the bank. Tangible assets are real, touchable objects, such as inventory, equipment, money, and tools. The opposite, intangible assets, cannot be touched but do have value. A regular clientele, an outstanding reputation, or a display at the Smithsonian would be intangibles. If the categories seem to overlap, give yourself an *A* for observation. The broad coverage is an accounting design to make certain everything of value gets included.

Liabilities means what you owe. Anything from the loan on your soldering iron to mortgage payments and payroll taxes would be included here. The difference between the two categories (assets and liabilities) is the "net worth" of your business.

Usually an accountant prepares the balance sheet, and you may think the service is well worth the investment. But balance sheets aren't complicated, so this is one area where you can save by doing it yourself. Anyone who can get through a long form at tax time can handle a balance sheet for a small business.

Recordkeeping will be expedited if you rely on certain standard procedures to document your business transactions. Make an excursion to your local office-supply store and open your world to the preprinted forms available to make these jobs easier. There is one for almost every need. Some basic forms you will probably be dealing with are purchase orders, packing slips, invoices, and statements.

If you've waited a lifetime to see your name in print, here's your big chance. Order forms with your name and address imprinted, or purchase a rubber stamp and personalize them yourself. (The rubber stamp is the cheaper way.) And while you're at it, order some stationery with a personalized letterhead and some business cards. It looks so professional.

Now that you have them, start using them. When a customer wants to buy one of your items before you're ready to hand it to him, you will detail his request on a *purchase order*. This is to make sure you and he understand each other. Include a description of each item (with catalog number, if there is one), price, payment terms, delivery date, where it is to be shipped, and who pays for shipping. Be sure to buy purchase order forms with space to write special information such as which items are out of stock and will be sent later, where the merchandise is to be shipped if the address differs from the one to be billed, if there's to be a cancellation date if the delivery cannot be made on time, and special handling or packaging instructions. Fill out the order in duplicate, giving one to the customer and keeping one for your files.

If you will be sending the merchandise to the buyer, enclose a *packing slip* in the package. This slip should identify only the merchandise in the package. Include one slip with each box. If the order is incomplete, the buyer can see at a glance where he's short by comparing the packing slip to his purchase order.

Packing slips provide a kind of instant inventory for the receiver and a double check for the sender. It is not a bill.

After the customer has received the products, you send him an *invoice,* commonly known as a bill. It lists what he has purchased and requests payment. The invoice should include all pertinent information about what was sold. Begin by numbering it. (Some invoices come prenumbered.) The number gives both you and the customer a reference to a specific order. Then proceed to fill in the blanks: date, your name, address, and phone, the customer's name and address, where the merchandise was sent and how (UPS, COD), and return and damage stipulations. (Some sellers will pay shipping damages only if notified within ten days of the receipt of the merchandise and returns only if within five days.)

Most important are the descriptions of the objects you've sold. If they have stock numbers, use them. Include a price for each item, shipping charges, tax, and total. State payment terms. If there is to be a discount for prompt payment, say so. Standard payment terms are abbreviated 2/10–net 30. This means payment is due within thirty days, but you are offering a 2 percent discount if the bill is paid within ten days.

It's best to type the invoice if you can. Again, use duplicate forms. Keep a copy for your files and send the original to the customer.

A *statement* is a communication you send to all your regular customers, usually once a month. It is a recapitulation of all the transactions between you and the customer during that month. It lists everything that was ordered, plus the invoice numbers, adds any previous balance, and subtracts payments received. It ends with a current balance, which can be either an amount or "O," to indicate nothing is due. If the customer has overpaid, there will be a credit. In this case, the credit is applied to the next order. A statement does not request payment; it is simply a record of the customer's account, another effort at communication between you and the customer.

Now to organize all those papers. Buy a few dozen file folders and hunt up a cardboard box. Later you can invest in a metal file cabinet. The systems vary, but two basic plans work well. An alphabetical listing by contacts or products is one choice. The other is a numbered listing by accounts. Products or names are easier to remember, so most craftspeople opt for the ABC's. Label each folder, and then stuff it with everything pertaining to the label. It is advisable to date everything you file and attach little notes to orders, invoices, or statements if there's something you might forget. If you couldn't sell product X during the holidays, but found that it was a hot number around the fourth of July, a note for future orders will remind you when stock choices are being made. You also might want to keep a front-page statement sheet in each folder so you'll know at a glance where you stand with each customer.

Mississippian Sandra Porter has developed her own method of keeping records straight. She has two large cartons, one red, one black. Paid-up files are stashed in the black box; ones with money owing go in the red one. She goes through the red carton at the middle and end of every month, pays the bills she owes, and sends bills to those owing her. When bills come in, she puts them in the proper folder and puts the folder in the red box. Sandra says, "it's fun—more like a game than work. I'm always trying to get all the folders in the black box."

You will, of course, adapt a system that works for you. Filing systems, like personalities, are unique to each individual.

Another helpful bit of paperwork is a card file of contacts. Office supply shops carry all kinds of neat gadgets for this, but you can get by with an alphabetized pile of 3 × 5 cards held together with a rubber band. Record names, addresses, and phone numbers of suppliers, show managers, your accountant, lawyer or tax man, and anyone else contacted on a regular basis. All of these notations systematically filed can save hours of searching.

There are good reasons for keeping accurate records. One is to be able to prove you're a good credit risk. Another is to let you know where you stand. You can see a glance how much business you're doing, the kinds of expenses you're running up and if they're too high, what you owe and who owes you, whether you're running in the black or the red, where your capital is tied up, and what's in the bank. If you're looking for trends, profit makers, or reliable suppliers, your books will talk to you.

The main reason for keeping meticulous records is that they will be essential at tax time. As long as you have a "profit motive," and the IRS defines that as earning more than you spend on your business in at least two out of five years, you can subtract your expenses before you pay taxes on your business income. Therefore, an accurate account of all your deductible expenses is essential. The IRS isn't interested in your good word—keep all receipts.

According to the IRS, deductible expenses are those that are "ordinary" and "necessary" to the operation of your business. This includes supplies, advertising, rent, insurance, utilities, professional journals, postage, travel, depreciation on equipment, legal and other professional fees, employee's wages, educational expenses to further your skills, and even baby sitting if it's needed to enable you to work.

If you rent a studio or shop, it's easy to determine your overhead simply by adding up rent and utility receipts. If you operate out of your home, it's a bit more complicated. You are entitled to deduct a percentage of your total household expenses equal to the percentage of your home used for your business. For instance, if two out of eight rooms in your house are used exclusively for the production, storage, and/or marketing of your craft, you may deduct one fourth of all your total annual heating and electric bills. Telephone too. If one fourth of all your calls are business related, 25 percent of the basic bill plus all business-related long distance calls can be written off. List and calculate all other expenses for occupying space in your home. Don't forget rent, property insurance, and maintenance. If you own your home, you can deduct for a percentage of the property taxes (if you haven't already accounted for them on your personal income tax form) and depreciation on the house.

But be careful. Since 1976 the IRS has been very stringent in allowing deductions, for home offices and studios. To qualify for these deductions the section of your home designated for business must be used for no other purpose than business and must be your principal place of doing business. If your home shop is used occasionally as a playroom or family room, it does not qualify for the deductions. Likewise, if your home studio is not your *principal* place of doing business, even if the room is used for no other purpose, you may not deduct it.

How do you keep track of all of these expenses? Grab some more of those file folders. Label each with an expense category, such as "supplies," or "promotions," etc. Whenever you get a receipt, toss it into the appropriate folder. You won't need to look at them again until tax time.

Significant purchases, such as a delivery van or lathe—anything that will last for more than a year—are not eligible for a full deduction in the same way that depletable supplies are. Such writeoffs are subject to depreciation and are bound by a separate kind of system. Most craftspeople use one of two. The more popular is the straight-line method. To compute the amount to deduct annually, refer to an IRS table to determine the expected life of your item. It might be a potter's wheel with a ten-year life. If the wheel put you back $300, this figure is divided by the life of the wheel, and equal annual amounts are deducted over the lifetime period—in this case, $30 each year for ten years.

The declining-balance method is choice two. A predetermined percentage is used to devalue the object annually, and you declare each year's loss as a deduction. Using the same $300 kiln and a 10-percent figure, the first year it loses 10 percent of its value, so you can declare a $30 loss. It is now worth $270. The following year you declare 10 percent of its present value, which is $27. The kiln is now worth $243. The third year you deduct $24.30, leaving a $218.70 kiln. You continue to declare 10 percent of the remaining balance each year until the entire sum has been consumed.

If a piece of equipment (or fixed asset) has personal as well as business use, the deduction must reflect only the percentage of business use. A sewing machine may produce your craft, but sewing for the family as well is not deductible.

Equipment that wears out sooner or lasts longer than specified on the IRS table is not eligible for special consideration. But if you want to get rid of equipment before its "life" is up, check the back of Form 3468 and Publication 572 on Tax Information and Investment Credits for an explanation on procedures for trading, selling, and replacing stolen or damaged assets.

Just as all bookkeeping procedures most follow the same format from year to year, depreciation claims must be done consistently. If you change your mind and switch from the straight-line to declining-balance method, you must file Form 3115 within ninety days from the start of the tax year.

Travel and entertainment expenses come quickly to mind when deductions are being listed. Since this area is often challenged and sometimes difficult to prove, keep careful and explicit records. There are preprinted forms for this at the office supply shop, but a 3 × 5 card in the glove compartment will do. Record the amount, location, date, and purpose of each trip or event you plan to declare. Travel to fairs, shows, the library, and suppliers all count. If it's business-related, mark it down. Expenses include transportation costs (if it's your own car, figure $.15 per mile for the first fifteen thousand miles, $.10 per mile thereafter), meals, lodging, tips, phone calls, even valet service.

Proving that your trip is worthy of a deduction requires some planning. If you're exhibiting in New York City and intend to meet with buyers while there, write ahead of time. Share your schedule. Make copies of the letters, and—bingo!— proof of the business intended by the trip. You might even entertain while on a business trip. Collect receipts to prove where you were. Be sure to date the slips and state the amount spent, the business purpose, and the name and business relationship of each person entertained.

Business and pleasure can be combined as long as you don't mix up the receipts. A week at an arts festival in San Diego followed by a week on the beach is fine. Mileage coming and going is deductible; the rented beach towel is not.

Your travel expenses need a folder just like everything else. Label it. Chuck in the information, and chalk up another bag of deductions.

When it comes time to spill the bag and sort through the files, you'll appreciate your records. Poet T. S. Eliot called April "the cruelest month of all." Maybe he had to do his own taxes too. Doing yours will be easier when you can defend the deductibles.

Schedule C is what you use if you're a sole proprietor (partnerships use 1065). Although the form is not long, it may seem confusing at first. There might be a question about Line A, which asks for the principal business activity and the type of product. If you sell mainly at shows and fairs, you are a retailer, and your product could be jewelry, pottery, clothing, or sculpture. If you sell a variety of products, your business activity is whichever item brings in the most money. Wholesaling goes on Line A if you sell most of your wares directly to stores. Line C requests an employer identification number. Persons who sell alcohol, tobacco, or firearms have this number. It doesn't affect many craftspeople.

If you get bogged down, the IRS has a number of free publications to help you. Ask for Publication 333, Tax Guide for Small Businesses; 535, Tax Information and Business Expenses; and 463, Travel, Entertainment and Gift Expenses. You can also purchase an income tax guide at the bookstore for a couple of dollars (deductible, of course!) which you'll probably find easier to understand than the government publications.

If you still need help, phone your questions to the IRS.

Listings and toll-free numbers are under "United States Government" in the directory. There is no need to identify yourself or your company. Their offices are open during regular business hours to assist taxpayers in filing their returns. Also, if you think an item you've declared might need further explanation, it's all right to attach a note to your tax form.

You see your profit in print on Line 21, the bottom line of Schedule C. Put this figure under "other income" on your 1040 income tax form. It is possible to have a negative profit figure. Many times craftspeople run in the red during the first year or two. When this happens, you can deduct this from your other income on your 1040. But watch it. Early in the chapter it was mentioned that you must be profit motivated to retain a business status with the IRS. You must make a profit in two out of every five consecutive business years to remain eligible to claim business deductions.

If you are fully self-employed, there's another form of file along with your annual income tax: Schedule 1040 SE, the self-employment social security tax form. Social security (FICA) tax amounts to 7.9 percent of your net income up to $16,500. The most you'll pay is $1,303.50. You pay this tax on self-employment income even if you already receive social security benefits. If you have another job, and your employer has already withheld the maximum FICA taxes, you won't need to worry about paying again. Also, you don't need to file if you earn under $400 a year.

When the amount of your tax is transferred to the 1040 form (line 55), the government will credit your social security account. And when retirement time arrives, you can collect social security and Medicare benefits.

If you don't have an employer to withhold a regular amount

from each paycheck to cover what you'll owe Uncle Sam, you'll have to file an estimated quarterly return (ES). Basically, this entails estimating what your annual income, after expenses, will be, figuring your tax on this amount, and dividing by four. Your taxes must then be paid in quarterly installments, on the fifteenth of April, June, September, and January.

If you are employed elsewhere, simply have your employer withhold enough extra to cover your self-employment income. Then you won't have to file the estimated quarterly return. As long as the government has your money, they don't much care how it got there.

If you're getting started, you're probably wondering how you can know how much you're going to make next year. That's understandable. There will be a lot of educated guesswork involved until you establish some averages, and even then you may never have an average year. Fortunately, you have three chances to make adjustments. Each time you send in your quarterly installment you can adjust the balance you owe. If you realize you're not going to make as much as you thought you were, simply credit yourself the excess on the remaining installments. If you've underpaied, it's more serious. You'll owe a penalty of 7 percent or more if you don't pay at least 80 percent of the total installment due. So, if it appears you're going to be pulling in substantially more than previously estimated, recalculate your estimated taxes and make up the deficit. It's better to overpay than underpay. You'll get a refund next April if you've got it coming.

Even though you've been diligent and efficient about filing taxes and maintaining your records, the day may come when the taxes can't be completed on time. The IRS provides. If you need an extension beyond the April fifteenth deadline, there is a form you can request to allow a delay (What a surprise, another form!). Number 4868 will allow an extension until June fifteenth. Incorporated businesses can do the same with Form 7004, and partnerships can join the Johnny-come-latelies with 2758.

The C, SE, and ES forms wrap it up for the individual. If it all seems too confusing, you can hire a tax expert to handle it for you, but chances are, once you've done it, it won't seem so overwhelming.

We've been assuming up to this point that you operate what is known as a sole, or single, proprietorship. Most beginners do opt for this form because of the simplicity of it. With such a setup you have no one to answer to, but also no one to fall back on. You can make all business decisions yourself, but you're limited by the extent of your own talents and abilities. As a sole proprietor, you and the business are considered one, and your financial risk goes beyond what you have invested in the business. Creditors can collect from your personal assets if there is not enough in the business to satisfy them. For the same reason, it may be difficult to expand your business, since your borrowing power is also limited by your own personal assets. And when you die, the business ceases to exist.

There are two other forms of operation that eliminate some of the drawbacks of the sole proprietorship, but they have their own headaches. These are the *partnership* and the *corporation*. Whether your address is your garage or Fifth Avenue, you will use one of these three forms of business. It will help to have an understanding of each in order to choose the form that best suits your needs.

If there's someone you'd like to go into business with, a

partnership may be for you. With such an arrangement two or more people are co-owners of the business.

Partners share profits and losses and have joint control over the management of the business and its assets. There are a couple of advantages of doing business this way: the combined net worth of the individual partners makes getting credit easier than it is for a single owner. And you can combine your talents to form a near-perfect blend. As with a good marriage, partners' skills can complement each other and offset each other's deficiencies. Combining your artistic talents with those of a good business head or customer cultivator can do much to stimulate sales.

Before entering a partnership, however, find out the personal financial status of the other prospective partners. That's because in a partnership all partners have unlimited liability for the partnership's debts. That means that if the partnership cannot pay its debts, or is sued, creditors can come to *any* partner and attempt to satisfy their claims from his personal assets (as they can with a sole proprietor). The real problem comes when one partner does not have enough to cover his share of the loss. Then the creditors may go to the other partners to get their money, regardless of any previous agreement among the partners to share losses equally. Be aware of this risk if you plan to join up with someone with substantially limited means.

Besides knowing your partner's financial status, also be sure he or she is someone you can work with. As with any relationship, interpersonal conflicts are inevitable in a joint ownership arrangement, but you can keep them as low as possible by choosing wisely.

To form a partnership, usually all you have to do is file a

"certificate of co-partnership" with the county. But, while you're there, pick up a "partnership agreement" form so you and your partners can reduce all your understandings to writing. This agreement is not legally required, but it makes good sense. Too many disasters come from partners failing to make agreements—and put them in writing—before the business gets going. It's wise to enlist a lawyer at this stage.

When all partners are involved in the management of the business, we're talking about a general partnership. There's another form of partnership in which one or more partners contribute money but don't have anything to do with the actual operation of the business. This is a *limited partnership,* and the financial backer is called a limited, or silent partner.

Of such a set-up dreams are made—a wealthy sponsor sees promise in your talent and is willing to put up all of the capital to launch you in business. You contribute the skill and know-how; he contributes the money. It can work to the advantage of both. He receives a percentage of the profits and is liable for debts only up to his original investment. You start a business you could not have started otherwise.

Partnerships do not pay income taxes, but each partner pays personal income tax on his share of the profit. Your partnership must, however, file a "U.S. Partnership Return of Income" form, a four-page schedule from the IRS.

If you're ready to go into business in a big way, you might decide to become a corporation. Because it involves considerable time, effort, and expense and doesn't have much financial advantage to a craftsperson in the low-profit stages, incorporation is not usually for the beginner.

One of the main advantages to being a corporation is that you and the other stockholders (owners) are not personally liable for the business's debts. A stockholder has the same protection that a limited partner has: he cannot lose more than he invests. The corporation is a separate legal entity, distinct from its owners. In fact, the corporation goes on even if the owners die.

Another advantage, when profits are great enough to make it feasible, is that the corporation can pay all your fringe benefits: medical and life insurance, workmen's compensation, pension plans, even a company car. These are considered corporate expenses and are deducted from company profits before taxes are figured. And it's easy for a corporation to raise additional capital. All it has to do is sell more stock. Tax breaks such as these and legal ways to "hide" assets and build funds tempt many businesspeople to incorporate.

Unlike partnerships, corporations pay income tax. Profits left after salaries are taxed at 22 percent (26 percent on profits over $25,000). The employees then pay personal income tax on their salaries.

There's one form of corporation which may interest you if you want to start small. It's a *Sub Chapter "S"* corporation. Generally, this form of corporation is not taxed. Instead, its income or losses are considered to be the income or losses of its shareholders. Sub Chapter "S" corporations are small, having no more than ten shareholders, but they have all the normal corporate advantages.

Incorporation has many advantages you might overlook, many legal complexities you could botch up, so unless you're really into all the ramifications of starting and operating a corporation, it is wise to enlist the help of a lawyer or an accountant, or both.

The attorney's job is to inform you about corporation legal

requirements, the responsibilities and powers of stockholders and directors, the ins and outs of contracts, and problems for small claims courts, as well as copyright, zoning, and distribution laws. If there are lawsuits or other situations in which you need legal counsel, he will interpret, represent, and if necessary, defend the interests of the corporation.

Why not do it yourself? You probably can until trouble arises. It's like treating yourself medically. Nothing prevents you from diagnosing and treating your own illness, but if it becomes serious and requires hospitalization, you cannot admit yourself and prescribe your own treatment. Only a trained physician is capable, or permitted, to do that. In the business world only bar-accepted, practicing attorneys can fight the battles of a corporation.

While the lawyer will guide you through tax laws, your accountant will take you through the numbers maze. This professional can set up an easily maintained bookkeeping system, one in which you write your own checks and keep the bank books balanced. He will also prepare annual tax and stockholders' reports.

Or you can hire a firm to handle your accounting problems. Accounting firms can also be hired to write checks, maintain payroll records, note employee tax withholdings, and provide monthly or quarterly statements.

The professionals needed by the corporation can be found in the yellow pages or through your banker, professional organizations, or friends in the field. It's worth shopping around to find one who will do the jobs you need done at a price within your means. Be sure to get someone who is oriented to small businesses.

If the services are not in this year's budget, don't despair.

Organizations, such as BALA (Bay Area Lawyers for the Arts) in Berkeley, California, offer free or inexpensive legal services to craftspeople in most urban areas. The Small Business Administration can guide you to them. Your public library, county bar association, and city municipal staff will also have information to direct you to help in getting your business off the ground.

Whether or not you retain a lawyer, there are a few laws relating to the sale of crafts items you should know about. Some protect you, others are designed to protect your customers. Copyrights and patents are for you. In this xerox age when handworked goods can be easily copied and cheaply produced, *copyrighting* helps to limit the use of your design. It protects your originality. Your copyright is a legal certificate and is the basis to sue when your idea has been stolen. Slick Grabber will be less likely to steal your idea if he knows a lawsuit is possible.

For a mere $10 you can copyright your creative works for your lifetime (plus fifty years). Going about it is simple. Send for an application (Form G) from Register of Copyrights, Library of Congress, Washington, DC 20540. Each article you copyright must be filed separately. Along with your application and fee the government requires two copies, photographs, or prints of the product. The certificate of copyright will take a few months to process.

The Library of Congress bulletin "General Information on Copyright," Circular I, states that any "works of art, models, or designs for workers of art" can be copyrighted if they are decorative rather than useful, functional, or mechanized. If you are considering copyrighting your product, however, ask yourself how easy it would be for someone to copy your idea. It may be worth the effort to copyright an easily duplicated piece of jewelry or a simply designed knit carryall, but there is little need to copyright one-of-a-kind wall-sized weavings or hand-carved figurines.

If you'd like protection for a new device you've discovered for firing ceramics, a new mixture or method for your glazes, or a new and original design for a *functional* object, you'd apply for a *patent* rather than a copyright. For example, if you took a conventional toaster and designed a casing which looked like a volcano, you'd want a design patent. If you created a volcano sculpture with no toaster inside, a copyright would do.

Patent protection is more complicated and expensive to acquire than copyrights. You'll need careful documentation of your creation. The patent office will make a search to see if anyone else has registered your brainchild. This can cost from $100 to several hundred dollars. Applying for a patent requires a lot of legal work that should be handled by a patent attorney. This assistance will probably cost you at least $1000. You'll have to decide if your "invention" is likely to produce enough money to justify this effort and expense.

Copyrights and design patents go into effect "on publication," that is, when the work is ready to be sold. To give you a legal leg to stand on, each item must be labeled with your copyright or patent information. This includes the word copyright or the symbol ©, your name, and the first year of publication. If you are Sue Silversmith with a 1975 first publication date, your copyright would look like this: © Silversmith, 1975. This information must be on the article itself, not on an attached tag or label. If you release catalogs, pamphlets, or flyers that include photographs or illustrations of your pieces, and the copyright data aren't visible, add them somewhere in the literature.

Another way to label your work is with a *trademark*. An

eye-catching, highly stylized design is one way of selling your goods on the basis of your reputation. You can create and use your trademark without registering it. The advantage of registering it is that no one else can use it. This prevents customers from confusing the source of your productions.

To file, the article must already be in interstate commerce (sold in more than one state). The application is $35, and the form is acquired from the Patent and Trademark Office, Washington, DC 20231. With the application, five samples or photographs of how the trademark is used and a drawing of the trademark are needed. A government pamphlet, "General Information Concerning Trademarks," is available from the Superintendent of Documents, US Government Printing Office, Washington, DC 20402, for $.50. It's worth the money if you're anxious to establish your image.

The laws aren't all in your favor. There are laws to protect your customers, too. There are textile acts, flammability acts, metal content acts, pottery usage acts, and paint regulations, to name just a few. The list is long, the legislation ever-changing. Write to the Federal Trade Commission, Pennsylvania Avenue at 6th, NW, Washington, DC 20580, and your state health department (listed in the phone book) for information about your particular product. You have nothing to lose by checking it out and perhaps a lawsuit to spare.

As soon as you start out selling your crafts, you should have already begun thinking about insurance. You probably already have some car, life, medical, hospital, and homeowner's or property insurance. As a craftsperson you will need some additional coverage for your specialized needs.

If you're still at the hobby stage, it is doubtful that your investment warrants greatly increasing your present coverage, but if you are totally dependent on your craft to earn your living, you'd better be sure you are covered to the full replacement value of your materials, tools, and inventory.

What else? Huntington T. Block, notable art insurance expert of Washington, DC, recommends "wall-to-wall coverage." By this he means covering everything you own, purchase, create, shelve, store, loan, show, or consign. It should include fire (don't skimp here), theft, water damage, shipping, life, disability, personal, product, and public liability coverage.

If you're well heeled and heavily invested, go "wall-to-wall." But if you're still on the starting block, you don't need to get bogged down in coverage. Get some advice from a competent, independent insurance broker as to what level of coverage is sensible for you at this point. Local crafts organizations can usually recommend a professional acquainted with the field. If you must choose blindly, ask your contacts if they are familiar with the insurance needs and problems of small businessmen or, better yet, craftspeople.

One rule of thumb should guide you: If you can't live or work without it, insure it. A potter's kiln or a weaver's loom are vital to the production of your craft. It's ridiculous to assume the risk yourself. Beyond that, it's up to you. Common sense should be the key.

If you transport your crafts to shows and fairs, you'd be wise to add a *fine arts floater* to your property insurance policy. This is a separate attachment to your existing policy which covers your goods during transit and while being stored or exhibited away from your property. Such coverage is also good for shipping and is advisable for craftspeople who consign.

If you have customers coming into your home or shop, you will need *public liability* insurance in case anyone should be injured on your premises and decide to sue.

Product liability is something else to consider. This is to protect you in case a defect in your product causes injury to a user. If your pot breaks while a buyer uses it to boil spaghetti, and he should become severely burned, you might have a lawsuit on your hands.

One way to avoid product defect lawsuits is to label your products as to proper care and usage and expected wearability and durability. Protesting that, "I never said it would cook spaghetti," is not enough when someone has you in small claims court. If it's ovenproof, say so. If not, label it FOR DECORATIVE USE ONLY. Your liability insurance will cover you in the event of a lawsuit, but why take a chance? Describing the limits of your craft is free insurance. You can't afford not to invest in it.

Once your goods are covered, look after yourself. If you're self-employed, you need *disability* coverage against the possibility of your becoming too sick or injured to work. Unfortunately, this type of insurance is hard to get unless you're incorporated. If you're not incorporated, you can attempt to get disability insurance by joining an organization, such as the American Crafts Council, and taking advantage of their group rates. And there are a few insurance companies that will provide such coverage, often with deductible rates.

If you're in a partnership, you might be able to work out an arrangement with your partners to provide disability income if one of the partners needs it. When Tom Hexamer joined his friend Pete Rosedale to open a shellcraft business in Florida, they wrote a contract that allowed either partner to collect income during any six-week period if a disability or illness should occur. Soon after his arrival, Tom developed an asthmatic condition that put him out of work temporarily. During his absence Tom and his family had an income, and through Pete's efforts, the business remained productive. Such agreements, of course, need to be worked out long before accident time and should be part of your partnership agreement.

If nothing can be worked out (and this is a pretty good possibility), bank a disability fund for yourself. A three-month fund is ideal, but a month's income is good for starters. Even a week or a day is better than nothing.

It's extremely important to have some *medical* coverage as well. If you or your spouse work for a company that has group coverage, this is no problem, but individual rates can be very high. If you're self-employed, you can ease the burden slightly by getting only major coverage and keeping enough in your savings to cover minor emergencies. You can save further by finding a group plan that you can get into. Many associations offer such plans to members and their families. The American Crafts Council is one. It offers group rates for major medical and hospital indemnity coverage. This reason alone might make it worth your while to join such an organization.

There's one more stitch for your security blanket: a *pension plan* of some sort. Even if retirement seems a long way away, such plans need to begin years, even decades before they're needed.

If you're self-employed, you can put away funds in either a Keogh or an IRA (Individual Retirement Account) plan. With either plan you can contribute up to 15 percent of your income and won't have to pay tax on the money until it is withdrawn, when you'll probably be in a lower tax bracket than you are now. The only significant difference between the two plans is the maximum total amount that can be put away each year. With the Keogh plan it's $7,500, and with the IRA,

$1,500 ($1,750 if your spouse is not employed). You can set up an IRA account even if you're not self-employed if you work for a company that has no pension plan. The Keogh plan, however, is strictly for the self-employed. Either choice should be considered permanent. Money deposited can't be withdrawn until you're at least 59½ years old (or totally disabled or die) without paying substantial penalties. In addition to paying regular income tax on the amount withdrawn, you'll have to add 10 percent of the amount withdrawn to the total income tax you owe for that year.

A retirement account can be set up with most banks, savings and loan associations, and credit unions. But before you finalize a decision, talk to a banker or accountant. Consider the advantages and disadvantages of such a plan over other forms of investment, and study the IRS publications "Retirement Plans for Self-Employed Individuals" (560) and "Questions and Answers on Retirement Plans for the Self-Employed" (566).

When your business feet are firmly and healthfully planted, and your operation is flourishing, the day may come when the front desk demands too much of your time. The crafting is suffering. To correct this you'll probably hire someone to take your place at either the desk or the workbench.

When help arrives, the paperwork mushrooms. First you will need an employer identification number. You get this by filling out an application from the IRS. It takes four to six weeks to process. You will be required to withhold income tax and social security tax from the employee's wages and to pay unemployment tax and your portion of social security tax out of your own funds. (The employee pays a 5.85 percent of his salary, up to $16,500, for social security, and you match that sum.) Forms for these tasks and publications to explain them are available at the IRS office. You're going to need forms W2, W3, W4, 940, and 941. All the forms are filed just once a year, except 941, which is for your quarterly social security tax payment, and W4, which is filled out by each employee only once.

While you're at it, check state and local tax offices for their requirements. The Department of Labor, which is located in your state capitol, will furnish information about employee taxes, minimum wage statutes, and other regulations that are unique to your state.

The responsibilities surge on . . . Each employee should have a personnel file. Include his job application, resume or previous work record, job references, salary schedule, and pay increases. A record of earnings and employment sheet are necessary and can be bought as a preprinted form at office supply stores.

Sounds like you'll need an employee just to help you recover from having hired an employee! But it should come as no surprise that the government requires you to write everything down.

Fringe benefits are another consideration. If you're a corporation, chances are the corporation is paying your benefits, such as medical coverage, life insurance, retirement plans, even a company car or plane (wow!), so that you can claim a lower salary, lower company profits, and thus pay less income tax. Naturally. Everybody likes fringe benefits and lower taxes. But if you have employees, IRS says you must offer the same benefits to them that you take for yourself, as owner of the business. This will probably keep you from getting too carried away in fringe benefits.

You can save yourself a lot of red tape if you can hire an assistant on a free-lance basis. It isn't how many hours the person works nor how much you pay that determines his status as employee or subcontractor, it's the arrangement you and he work out. With an employee, you set the working conditions—hours, days, pay, benefits, holidays, and provide work space and supplies. You also fill out all those papers and pay taxes. With a subcontractor or free-lance assistant, the worker offers to do a set job for a set fee as a self-employed person. He may provide his own work space and supplies (you arrange this between you), sets his own hours, and receives no benefits from you. He submits a bill to you for services rendered, you pay him, and that's that. He takes care of his own quarterly estimated income tax and social security taxes. To reach this kind of agreement with an assistant, you may have to offer slightly higher wages to make up for the lack of employee benefits.

There are ways to learn the business side of crafting without doing it the hard way. Working in someone else's craft shop is one. You can gain experience with bookkeeping as well as other aspects of retailing at someone else's expense. Another is to take a course or two at a community college or adult education program sponsored by your local schools. Coursework might include accounting, general or business bookkeeping, business law, and tax preparation. Any course with the words "small business" in the title should help you. The government has over eighty small business administration field offices all over the country that can answer a novice's questions. And many city directories list SCORE organizations (Service Corps of Retired Executives), whose members are eager to help. These former businesspeople, accountants, salespeople, and executives have a lifetime of information to share and the time to share it. A goal of SCORE is to help the small businessperson get started and keep going. Chapter Eleven lists additional sources of help.

Plan, form, tax, deduction, record. Surviving it all will soon become a habit. With a well-organized set of books and regular attention, the at-first overwhelming trauma of pencil work and paperwork will soon give way to a flowing system. The key is in setting it up, maintaining it, and then watching it perform for you. Your craft may have put you in business, but your books will keep you there.

CHAPTER ELEVEN

Cooperation Pays

At its best crafts selling provides you with a sense of independence, but at its worst, it isolates you from community and even your craft work. Alone you may not be privy to crafts events in your region, and you'll have to learn which promoters and shopkeepers to avoid by painful experience. Alone you must spend endless hours away from your art in marketing and attending to endless business details. And by yourself you can expect to pay top dollar, usually full retail price, for your materials and equipment. Independence definitely has its price.

Yet there is a way of keeping most of that cherished independence while reaping the benefits of a large business operation. You can band together with other craftspeople in a democratically-controlled organization. Craft cooperatives, guilds, and associations can do many things for you that you can't, or don't care to, do on your own. These organizations can market your work, provide you with supplies at the lowest possible cost, offer training programs to upgrade your skills, and most important, develop a sense of community so often lacking in a lonely craft.

On the most elementary level, we are simply suggesting

cooperation with a few friends. Just get together over coffee in one of your homes and talk crafts. Pool your supply needs, thereby reaping the price advantage of large-quantity wholesale ordering, or work out a deal to produce and distribute a crafts catalog together at a fraction of the cost of a one-person catalog. Once you realize the benefits of size, you may then wish to expand into a cooperative, guild, or association, or join an existing organization en masse.

To lump cooperatives, guilds, and associations together as if they were synonyms is perhaps misleading. Each is a distinct form designed to achieve a somewhat different end. Yet there is a commonality of purpose, a sense of service to the individual needs of member patrons. All have the potential to broaden your markets and lessen your individual burden, and each is worthy of consideration.

One way to separate the three forms of organization in your mind is to consider them from the point of view of degree of involvement. In general, the cooperative requires the greatest personal commitment and time, the guild requires less dedication, and an association demands little, if any, direct participation. Benefits, however, are normally correlated with commitments. A co-op can provide you with more services than a guild normally will, and the guild serves more of your needs than an association. Although such generalizations don't always hold true, and some associations provide more direct services than some co-ops, the yardstick is most often a good one. The more you're asked to commit to an organization, the more that organization is attempting to do for you. Only you can decide at what point service becomes stifling, and therefore, what organization is best for your distinct personality and needs.

Cooperatives are the most distinct form of group activity. A co-op is a business in which volunteer members join together to get quality goods and services more economically than the members could obtain independently. Co-ops can be formed to serve a single need, such as organizing art fairs or, more commonly, to provide a full range of services for their members.

Co-ops are nonprofit businesses. Each member invests a set amount in initiation fees and monthly dues, and at the end of the year all the organization's excess earnings are returned to the individual members. This end-of-year refund, called "patronage," assures that the cooperative will not lose sight of its primary purpose of serving member needs. The not-for-profit character of cooperatives is an essential aspect of this form of business, and both federal and state laws governing co-ops limit the return on investment of stockholders' capital. Also worth noting here is that the patronage refund is not taxable as corporate dividends, which is a distinct member advantage.

Another distinct co-op characteristic is its democratic control. One member–one vote is the standard. While many co-ops allow individual members to invest in more than one share of the business stock, the member still has only one vote in running the organization. Most co-ops of any size function as a representative democracy. Members elect a board of directors who set general policy and may hire and direct a professional manager. Monthly meetings and frequent elections ensure strong member control of policies.

The co-op, in many respects, looks like a democratic club, but it retains many of the legal advantages of a corporation. Like the corporation, a co-op must receive a charter, either under the state or through federal charter in the District of Columbia. Once it is a legal entity, the co-op has an identity of its own and will continue to exist after any individual member leaves. In sole proprietorships or partnerships the business ceases to exist when an owner pulls up stakes. This continuity of a co-op makes it somewhat easier to obtain financing, short-term loans, and provides the advantage of limited member liability. That is, if someone decides to sue the organization, the rank-and-file members can't be held accountable.

A craft cooperative can help you in several ways. Let's look at some of the more common services co-ops typically provide:

Marketing is the biggest assist. The co-op can operate a retail store and sell members' crafts at a greater profit to the craftsperson than he or she would get on store consignment. A craft co-op can also sponsor shows and fairs. Each member pays a small fee to cover expenses and does not have to submit to often usurious promoters' fees. Because the co-op can produce volume, it is in a position to obtain major contracts with mass merchandising stores. The high cost of direct mail advertising is no longer a barrier with the shared investment in a co-op.

Co-ops can work as well to market one-of-a-kind crafts as they can to move large numbers of small items. Often, an artist co-op rents a gallery and provides members with individual showings for a couple of weeks each year plus a common showing at least once a year. These fine-art co-ops act as a clearinghouse where the most discriminating buyers can find unique art and crafts items.

Supplies are another major reason for joining a co-op. Too often a craftsperson buys his or her material at hobby shops at retail prices, while selling the finished work at wholesale prices, which creates a profit squeeze. In a recent survey conducted by *The Working Craftsman* magazine, craftspeople rated buying directly from hobby shops as the least desirable means of supply. A co-op can buy directly from manufacturers in large-volume, often carload lots, for even greater savings to members. Also, buying through a co-op eliminates the retail sales taxes you'd normally have to pay on supplies. A co-op can obtain tax exemption certification through the state and forego the tax which, in many states, now adds on another 5 percent. It is not unusual for a craftsperson buying through a co-op to save 50 percent over retail prices of supplies. Naturally, the big advantage here is size of order, so homogeneous crafts co-ops, such as all weavers, or all potters, can make the best deals.

Commonly-owned equipment is yet another potential benefit of a co-op. Large looms of kilns require investments many individuals are not able to make. The co-op can buy and maintain such equipment for you. This, of course, also entails a central or communal workshop. Many craftspeople find such an environment stimulating and are amazed at the increase in productivity which comes from avoiding the distractions of working at home. Others prefer solitude when creating and may not find this co-op benefit to be a benefit at all.

Technical assistance is also offered in most co-ops. This is done either through a casual buddy system in which more experienced craftspeople share tips and shortcuts or through formal class sessions. The cooperative movement has always emphasized education, and most co-ops bring in guest lecturers and reprint significant articles and speeches for members.

Co-op education faces outward as well. The members feel a

duty to develop the public image of crafts to the immediate community and the larger regional public. With continuity, the co-op can develop firm relationships with members of the press, which is a tremendous "in" when a show date comes up or an individual member seeks publicity.

Participation is a keynote of cooperatives, and with the demand for democratic involvement, it is hard to avoid mixing with others. The relationship is casual and inevitably leads to fraternization and social relationships. Husbands and wives of craftspeople are drawn in at parties and social gatherings, and a feeling of community evolves. Such a group shares experiences with sales, promotions, techniques, innovations, and even tips on doing income taxes. The experience is educational and, for most, quite satisfying.

There is, of course, a negative side to cooperatives. Usually they require that you put in a certain number of hours per month clerking at the co-op store, making trips to a supplier, or doing some other necessary tasks for the group. This saves you and other members the cost of paid employees, but it can cut into your creative time. Also, many marketing co-ops require that you contract with them to sell a certain amount of your production through them. That's necessary for them to know they'll have a stock to sell, but it can limit your own marketing flexibility.

Yet if you decide there are more advantages than shortcomings to creating a co-op, you'll find you'll have plenty of help. For co-operation is a full-scale international movement which encompasses not only crafts, but virtually all forms of consumer goods and services. Several national organizations are set up to serve the cooperator. The best and largest is The Cooperative League of the United States. This is a cooperative that serves co-ops of all kinds. It has the most extensive lists of publications, pamphlets, and legal forms to help a co-op get started and stay going. If you're at all interested in setting up a co-op, the League is the place to begin your inquiry. Write to The Cooperative League of the United States, Inc., 1012 Fourteenth Street, NW, Washington, DC 20036, and they'll inundate you with information and insights.

The federal government also assists the development of cooperatives. They found a few years back that basic crafts require a great deal of individual effort, but very little capital investment, so they are used extensively for job development programs in disadvantaged areas. Isolated people, either in rural communities or isolated by poverty in the city can be taught to make basic crafts items and thus create a cottage industry that pays. And since crafts production requires mature characteristics, such as patience, experience, and skills, they are often used as income programs for senior citizens. Several federal agencies thus have helped in setting up crafts co-ops, often by supplying knowledgeable advisors and, in some cases, financing. The Farmers' Home Administration, USDA, has loaned over $200,000 to rural crafts co-ops, for example. United Nations agencies are equally interested in crafts co-ops and sponsor them within the emerging nations. The entire movement is reminiscent of Mahatma Gandhi's attempt to bring crafts works to the poorer castes of India.

The Sixties was the high point of government assistance to co-ops. The Office of Economic Opportunity (OEO) was established in 1964 by an act of Congress and given the authorization to help individuals organize cooperatives in moderate-and-low-income communities. Recently, the name was changed to Community Services Administration (CSA), which is now a part of ACTION. Grants can be given by CSA either to start a cooperative or operate one once it is going. But either way, a proposal must be written to request a grant. CSA provides assistance in writing grant requests, too.

The recession of the early Seventies drastically curtailed funding to the OEO, so while grants are harder to come by now than a few years ago, they are still available primarily to the hard-core poverty-area cooperatives. The information and advice CSA offers, however, is in far greater abundance. Because Jimmy Carter is a long-time farm cooperator and supporter of CSA action, this agency may soon be revitalized with adequate funding.

Because the government sponsorships go to disadvantaged people to set up crafts co-ops in places like Appalachia, the deep South, and among Indians in the Southwest, there isn't much chance of getting money for a middle-class co-op. These organizations, however, have produced a mountain of materials on how to set up and operate a cooperative. By writing for their publications lists and ordering a few inexpensive books and booklets, you can obtain everything you need to know about crafts co-ops. Here are the organizations you should write:

National Council of the Aging
1828 L Street, NW
Washington, DC 20006

Special Projects Branch
Office of Education
Department of Health, Education, and Welfare
400 Maryland Avenue, SW
Washington, DC 20202

Education Division
National Trust for Historic Preservation
740 Jackson Place
Washington, DC 20006

Interior Planning and Design
General Services Administration
18th and F Streets, NW
Washington, DC 20405

Federal Coordination Branch
Rural Development Service
US Department of Agriculture
Washington, DC 20250

American Crafts Council
29 West 54th Street
New York, NY 10019

American Federation of Arts
41 East 65th Street
New York, NY 10021

Federal Inter-Agency Craft Committee
National Endowment for the Arts
Washington, DC 20506

The Office of Economic Opportunity
Office of Technical Assistance
Washington, DC 20506

Farmer Cooperative Service
U.S. Department of Agriculture
Washington, DC 20250

Indian Arts and Crafts Board
Room 4004
US Department of the Interior
Washington, DC 20240

If you live in Canada, you have no fewer sources of information and assistance on co-ops than you would in the United States. Both the national and provincial governments are active supporters of the co-op movement. The Cooperative Union of Canada (CUC) is the Canadian counterpart of The Cooperative League of the US. Established in 1909, CUC maintains a liaison between regional cooperatives and the Canadian Parliament. It has an educational function similar to CLUSA's, providing publications and booklets on all aspects of cooperation. A parallel organization, Le Conseil Canadien de la Cooperation (CCC), exists for French-speaking Canadians, but works closely with CUC activities. The official publication, *The Canadian Co-operator,* is well worth reading. For information write to Cooperative Union of Canada, 111 Sparks St., Ottawa, Ontario, Canada, IiP 5B5.

Guilds serve many of the same functions as co-ops, but there is an essential difference in their approach. For the centuries in which guilds have flourished, they have been the keepers of high professional standards. European guilds not only evaluate the quality of members' work, but dictate a prescribed route of professional development from apprentice to journeyman to master. Crafts guilds in the United States generally retain the emphasis on professionalism.

The Southern Highland Handicraft Guild is perhaps the best, and most typical example, of how a guild works. The applicant to Southern Highland must submit five samples of his or her best work. The Guild committee judges the quality of the designs, and if they are found to be professional, the individual is accepted into the organization. And even after acceptance, the Guild evaluates the craftsperson's work each time it is submitted to maintain the standards.

Because of quality standards, guilds are usually kept small. The Southern Highland Handicraft Guild, for example, is perhaps the largest in this country with no more than five hundred members. Yet because of the size and homogeneous skill levels of its members, guilds can provide numerous services. Guilds normally sponsor from two to four fairs a year and publish a top-quality catalog for members.

Guilds do a great deal in the member education area. They publish newsletters or even full-scale magazines and often conduct original research into craftspeople's needs and markets. They also benefit the self-employed craftsperson with group insurance, medical coverage, and information on retirement plans.

Unlike co-ops, guilds seldom bind their members to producing set quantities or selling through the organization. Guilds are usually more loosely joined institutions which members can use while remaining completely free from commitments beyond the basic dues. For the established craftsperson, this is a distinct advantage. But the beginner often finds that the co-op can provide more forms of initial assistance and group encouragement.

Associations are the most vaguely defined groups of all. Generally, they exist to encourage and support a definable group or art field. Unlike guilds and co-ops, membership is typically wide open not only to craftspeople but to anyone who has an interest in the subject. There is no real member commitment beyond dues, and meetings are infrequent and rarely attended. The associations strive for size, and most cover regions or the entire nation. To become a member, then, is more like belonging to a national fraternal organization or alumni group. You are simply a supporter of a cause.

Although of little assistance in direct marketing, associations do provide quite a few member services. They often represent the interests of the artists by employing lobbyists in Washington, DC, and state capitols. They produce magazines that keep the craftsperson informed on current issues and activities, and they occasionally sponsor educational seminars and conventions.

One of the most respected associations nationally is the *American Crafts Council.* Founded in 1943 as a nonprofit educational and cultural organization, the main thrust of ACC activities has been to stimulate interest in contemporary crafts. The organization is open to anyone and is supported entirely by dues and contributions.

Craft Horizons, the bimonthly magazine published by ACC since 1942, presents many aspects of craftsmanship, including coverage of national and international events in the arts. The Research and Education Department of ACC maintains a unique portfolio system of pictorial and biographical data on contemporary American craftspeople and operates a nationwide slide sales/rental service known as "Your Portable Museum." It publishes the *ACC Directory of Craft Courses, Craft Shops/Galleries USA,* and other references on crafts in all media, which can be seen in the ACC library at 44 West 53rd Street, New York, NY, or purchased by mail. Through the Council's Regional Program, fairs, workshops, and other educational projects are carried out under the aegis of regional assemblies of craftspeople from the fifty states. ACC maintains the Museum of Contemporary Crafts in New York City where the work of established and emerging artists in a variety of crafts media can be seen. For more information on ACC, write to them at 44 West 53rd Street, New York, NY 10019.

Associations and guilds rarely have the chance to obtain government financing under anti-poverty programs as do the cooperatives. But there are other federal agencies that make a concerted effort to encourage all participants in the arts and crafts realm. Government's rationale for involvement in crafts is many-faceted. As one federally-funded agency stated its reason for existence: "To make the arts more widely available to Americans, to preserve our rich cultural heritage for present and future generations ... and to encourage the creative development of our nation's finest talent," all of which are noble ends that most of us can readily appreciate.

The National Endowment for the Arts is just such an agency. With funding from Congress, the Endowment fund makes grants to organizations and individuals involved in the arts. The Endowment often makes grants of as much as $5,000 to an individual craftsperson or artist, and it makes considerably larger contributions (usually on a matching-funds basis) to cultural organizations. Information about grants is available by writing to Visual Arts Programs, National Endowment for the Arts, Washington, DC 20506.

The government has also made some effort to recognize the best in crafts through display, and sometimes sale, in national galleries. Renwich Gallery of the National Collection of Fine Arts, for example, displays not only fine arts, but decorative arts, crafts, and industrial arts. The Smithsonian Museum also buys American crafts and arts for display. And both Renwick and the Smithsonian have gallery gift shops where crafts judged of the highest quality are sold to the general public.

Both in the United States and Canada, local governments also make efforts to support crafts co-ops, guilds, associations, and lone craftspeople. Major cities and densely populated counties normally have an arts council which is completely or partially supported through public funds. Every state and Canadian province has an arts commission or council. Normally the state foots the bill for grants, loans, shows, and other methods used to develop local culture.

Like the federal government, state and local arts councils see their roles in various ways. The Crafts Council of New York State, for example emphasizes training and marketing for basic crafts largely to provide broader employment opportunities. Indiana has Operation Late Start, which trains senior citizens in crafts as income. Montana and New Mexico arts councils tend to see their work as perpetuating Indian crafts and Americana. And many other states see their function more as the aesthetic pursuit of fine arts.

To locate agencies and councils that can help you or your organization, simply write to the Associated Councils of the Arts, 570 Seventh Avenue, New York, NY 10018, for the complete list of state arts agencies. Your state agency can then put you in touch with county, city, and private organizations that are normally anxious to assist you. Because art forms appeal to the higher sensitivities of so many people, there is seldom a shortage of support for the individual who displays a real talent.

Neither this chapter, nor this book, can come to an end without connecting you up to the rich resources available through crafts magazines. Whether or not you feel the need to join a co-op, guild, or association you can hardly afford not to subscribe to one or more of the crafts magazines. They provide the full range of information on shows, catalogs, buyers, and other marketing opportunities, plus insightful advice from fellow craftspeople on working your art as well.

In recent years the crafts magazines have multiplied at a phenomenal pace, yet there is very little duplication in their efforts. Publications like *Handcrafters' News* zero in on selling methods and outlets, while others, like *Craft Horizons,* give primary attention to illustrating imaginative new or traditional designs. *The Crafts Report* is a monthly news publication that covers the business problems of craftspeople—marketing, management, and money. The crafts magazines often serve regional audiences, such as *Artweek* on the West Coast, *Craft Connection* in the Midwest, and *Sunshine Artists* with most of its subscribers in the South. Then, of course, there are the special skills magazines, such as *Needlepoint Arts, Rock and Gem, Studio Potter Magazine, Ceramic Review,* and *Fiber News,* whose names tell exactly what you can expect. At the end of this chapter, a list of crafts magazines will be provided. We strongly urge that you contact those which interest you and ask for sample copies and subscription details. Crafts magazines represent an extremely small cash outlay for a remarkably high dividend in information.

Becoming a professional craftsperson is really a matter of reaching out beyond the cloistered world of your own imagination. Through co-ops, guilds, associations, and publications you are touched by others, and for most of us, the process itself is inspirational. By making the effort to promote yourself, sell your work, and communicate your skill through teaching, you grow not only more prosperous but also more professional. If this book can leave you with only one thought, it is to reach out and get involved with others, for crafts are not entities, but functional aspects of a social existence. As Alexander Solzhenitzyn summed it up when he entered America: "Mankind's sole salvation lies in everyone making everything his business."

Listing of Crafts-Related Magazines

American Artist
Billboard Publications, Inc.
2160 Patterson Street
Cincinnati, OH 45214

American Candlemaker
P.O. Box 22227
San Diego, CA 92122

American Folklife
R.D. #2
Oley, PA 19547

American Home Crafts
641 Lexington Avenue
New York, NY 10022

Americana
1221 Avenue of the Americas
New York, NY 10020

Art Material Trade News
119 West 57th Street
New York, NY 10028

Art News
750 Third Avenue
New York, NY 10017

Artist and Handcrafter Information
    Service
P.O. Box 253
Burke, VA 22015

The Artist Magazine
817 Ringwood Avenue
Pompton Lakes, NJ 07442

Arts and Activities
8150 North Central Park Avenue
Skokie, Il 60076

Arts Magazine
23 East 26th Street
New York, NY 10010

Arts Management
The Radius Group
330 East 40th Street
New York, NY 10017

Artweek
1305 Franklin Street
Oakland, CA 94612

Art Workers News
The Foundation for the Community
    of Artists
220 Fifth Avenue
New York, NY 10001

The Bead Journal
P.O. Box 24C47
Los Angeles, CA 90024

Better Homes & Gardens Christmas
    Ideas
1716 Locust Street
Des Moines, IA 50336

Ceramics
Duncan Ceramic Products, Inc.
5673 East Shields Avenue
Fresno, CA 93727

Ceramic Arts & Crafts
Scott Advertising & Publishing Co.
30595 West 8 Mile Road
Livonia, MI 48152

Ceramics Monthly
1609 Northwest Blvd, Box 4548
Columbus, OH 43212

Ceramic Review
5 Belsize Lane
London NW3 5 AD England

Ceramic Scope
Box 48643
Los Angeles, CA 90048

Ceramic World
5905 Phinney Avenue, North
Seattle, WA 98103

Colorado Art Shows News
P.O. Box 609
Littleton, CO 80120

Counted Thread Society of Amer-
    ica Newsletter
3305 South Newport Street
Denver, CO 80222

Craft Connection
A Midwest Publication of the Min-
    nesota Crafts Council
900 Fairmount Avenue
St. Paul, MN 55105

Craft Dimensions Artisanales
Canadian Guild of Crafts
29 Prince Arthur Avenue
Toronto, Ontario M5R1B2 Canada

Craft Horizons
American Crafts Council
44 West 53rd Street
New York, NY 10019

Craft, Model & Hobby Industry
    Magazine
229 West 28th Street
New York, NY 10001

Crafts Fair Guide
Box 9132
Berkeley, CA 94709

The Craftsman's Gallery
Box 645
Rockville, MD 20851

The Crafts Report
1312 Third Avenue West
Seattle, WA 98119

Creative Crafts
Box 700
Newton, NJ 07860

Cultural Affairs
Associated Councils of the Arts
1564 Brooadway
New York, NY 10036

Decorating and Craft Ideas Made
    Easy
1001 Foch Street
Fort Worth, TX 76107

Design Magazine
1100 Waterway Blvd.
Indianapolis, IN 46202

Early American Life
P.O. Box 1831
Harrisburg, PA 17105

Embroidery
73 Wimpole Street
London W1M8AX England

Exhibit
P.O. Box 23505
Fort Lauderdale, FL 33307

Festival, USA
Superintendent of Documents
U.S. Government Printing Office
Washington, D.C. 20402

Fiber News
Handweavers Guild of
    America, Inc.

Art Department
Illinois State University
Normal, IL 61761

Fibernews
7201 Flora Morgan Trail
P.O. Box 619
Tujunga, CA 91042

Flying Needle
National Standards Council
    of American Embroiderers
1265 Southwest 300 Place
Federal Way, WA 98003

Fusion
American Scientific Glassblowers
    Society
309 Georgetown Avenue
Gwinhurst, Wilmington, DL 19809

Gems
The British Lapidary Magazine
84 Jigh Street
Broadstairs
Kent, England

Gems and Minerals
P.O. Box 687
Mentone, CA 92359

Glass
420 Governor Building
Portland, Oregon 97204

The Glass Workshop
482 Tappan Road
Northvale, NJ 07647

Good Housekeeping Needlecraft
959 Eighth Avenue
New York, NY 10019

The Goodfellow Review of Crafts
P.O. Box 4520
Berkeley, CA 94704

Handcrafters' News
808 High Mountain Road
Franklin Lakes, NJ 07417

Highland Highlights
Southern Highland Handicraft
   Guild
15 Reddick Road
Asheville, NC 29905

Hobbies
1006 South Michigan Avenue
Chicago, IL 60605

Hobbies & Things Magazine
30915 Loraine Road
North Olmstead, OH 44070

Hobby Potpourri
6531 Riverton
North Hollywood, CA 91606

Hobby World
5905 Phinney Avenue, North
Seattle, WA 98103

Interweave
2938 North Country Road 13
Loveland, CO 80537

Ladies' Home Journal Needle &
   Craft
641 Lexington Avenue
New York, NY 10022

Lady's Circle Home Crafts
Lady's Circle Needlework
21 West 26th Street
New York, NY 10010

Lapidary Journal
P.O. Box 80937
San Diego, CA 92138

Make It with Leather
(formerly The Craftsman)
P.O. Box 1386
Fort Worth, TX 76108

McCall's Needlework & Crafts
McCall's Christmas Annual
230 Park Avenue
New York, NY 10017

Mid-West Art
2025 East Fernwood Avenue
P.O. Box 4419
Milwaukee, WI 53207

Midwest Art Fare
Box 195
Garrison, IA 52229

National Calendar of
   Indoor/Outdoor Art Fairs
National Calendar of Open Art
   Exhibitions
5423 New Haven Avenue
Fort Wayne, IN 46803

National Carvers Museum Review
7825 South Claremont Avenue
Chicago, IL 60620

National Needlework News
2165 Jackson Street
San Francisco, CA 94115

National Sculpture Review
250 East 51st Street
New York, NY 10022

Near North News
26 E. Huron
Chicago, IL 60611

Needle Arts
Embroiderers' Guild
120 East 56th Street, Rm 228
New York, NY 10022

Needlepoint News
P.O. Box 668
Evanston, IL 60204

New York State
    Craftsmen/Bulletin
P.O. Box 733
Ithaca, NY 14840

Nimble Needle Treasures
The Quilters' Quarterly Magazine
Box 1082
Sapulpa, OK 74066

Nutshell News
1035 Nowkirk Drive
LaJolla, CA 92037

Olde Time Needlework Patterns
    and Designs
Tower Press, Inc.
Box 428
Seabrook, NH 03874

Open Chain
Newsletter for Thread Benders
632 Bay Road
Menlo Park, CA 94025

Ozark Mountaineer
Branson, MO 65616

Pack-O-Fun
14 Main Street
Park Ridge, IL 60068

Popular Ceramics
6011 Santa Monica Blvd.
Los Angeles, CA 90038

Popular Handicraft & Hobbies
Box 428
Seabrook, NH 03874

Profitable Craft Merchandising
News Plaza
Peoria, IL 61601

Quilter's Calendar
P.O. Box 270
Mill Valley, CA 94941

Quilters Newsletter
5315 West 38th Avenue
Wheatridge, CO 80033

Regional Art Fair List
Box 136, Rt. #1
Stockholm, WI 54769

Rock & Gem
16001 Ventura Boulevard
Encino, CA 91316

Rug Hookers News and Views
North Street
Kennebunkport, ME 04046

SCAN (Southern Crafts and Arts
    News)
Route 14, Box 571
Cullman, AL 35055

Shuttle, Spindle & Dyepot
1013 Farmington Avenue
West Hartford, CT 06107

Souvenirs and Novelties
20-21 Wagaraw Rd., Bldg. 30
Fairlawn, NJ 07410

Stained Glass
3600 University Drive
Fairfax, VA 22030

Stitch and Sew
P.O. Box 428
Seabrook, NH 03874

Studio Potter Magazine
Box 172
Warner, NH 03278

Sunshine Artists
Sun County Enterprises, Inc.
Drawer 836
Fern Park, FL 32730

Today's Art
25 West 45th Street
New York, NY 10036

Treasure Chest
411 Warren
Phillipsburg, NJ 08865

Tri-State Trader
P.O. Box 90
Knightstown, IN 46148

Westart
P.O. Box 1396
Auburn, CA 95603

Woman's Day Needlework Ideas
Woman's Day Knit and Stitch
1515 Broadway
New York, NY 10036

Woman's World Family Crafts
575 Madison Avenue
New York, NY 10022

Women's Circle Homeworker
Box 428
Seabrook, NH 03874

Workbasket
4251 Pennsylvania
Kansas City, MO 64111

Workbench
4251 Pennsylvania
Kansas City, MO 64111

The Working Craftsman
(formerly Craft/Midwest)
Box 42
Northbrook, IL 60062

INDEX

Advertising
  in direct mail sales
    brochures in, 77-78
    content of, 82
    of kits, 89-90
    mailing lists for, 75-77
  in media, 74-75, 78-81
Air freight, shipping via, 97-98
American Crafts Council
  insurance benefits of, 154, 155
  services of, 171-172
Apprenticeships, 102-103
Art fairs, profits in, 36
Artisans and Craftsmen, catalogs of, 83
Artists and Photographer's Market, 110
Arts and crafts
  distinction between, 11
  revival of, 1-3
Arts councils, function of, 173
Art therapy, 103-104
Assets, styles of, 134
Associations
  organization of, 170-171
  services of, 171-172
Ayer Directory of Publications, 80

Balance sheet, preparation of, 134
Bankruptcy, of new enterprises, 4
Barsness, John C., 123
Bookkeeping system, 133-134
Book presentations, 108
Business, *See* Crafts business
Business cards, 56
  design of, 125-126
  uses of, 125
Business name, registration of, 132
Bus lines, shipping via, 97-98
Buyers, presentations to, 68-71
By Hand: A Guide to Schools and a Career in Crafts, 103

Canada, craft cooperatives in, 169
Canadian Co-operator, 169
Catalogs
  application to, 85-86
  buying space in, 86
  examples, of 83, 84-85
  production of, 87-88
Catalog sales
  inventory commitment in, 86
  methods of, 83

pricing for, 84
Charge plans, subscription to, 57
COD delivery
  for crafts, 90
  by United Parcel Service, 97
  by US Post Office, 95
Collectors, of crafts, 16, 17
Colleges and universities, art programs in, 103
Commissions
  in craft shows, 57
  to sales representatives, 64, 65, 66
Common carrier, shipping via, 98
Community Services Administration (CSA), craft cooperative grants from, 166-167
Competition, comparison shopping with, 13-14, 22-23
Consignment forms, orders for, 43
Consignment selling
  benefits of, 37-38
  contract in, 41-43
  to galleries and museums, 44-48
  seasonal sales in, 48
  shop selection in, 38-40
Consignment shows, 54
Contacts, card file of, 138
Contemporary Crafts Marketplace, 103, 107
Contracts
  for consignments, 41-43
  in partnerships, 147
  with sales representatives, 65-66
Cooperative League of the United States, 165-166
Cooperative organizations, 160-161
Cooperatives
  benefits of, 163-165
  characteristics of, 162-163
  development assistance for, 165-167
  drawbacks of, 165
  information sources on, 167-169
Cooperative Union of Canada (CUC), 169
Copyrighting, procedure for, 150-151
Corporations
  accountants for, 149
  advantages of, 147-148
  fringe benefits in, 157
  legal services to, 148-149, 150
  taxation of, 148

Cost, per piece, 31
Cost calculation, 5
  formula for, 33
  labor in, 25, 28-30
  materials in, 25-27
  overhead in, 30-31
  profit in, 31-32
  selling expenses and, 32
Cost cutting, 33-34
Cottage industry, craftspeople in, 110-111
Crafts
  defined, 11
  design of, 12, 13-15
  interdisciplinary nature of, 12-13
  marketing of, 13-18
  pricing of, 21-36
  quality of, 18-19
  See also Arts and crafts
Crafts associations, cooperatives, guilds.
  See Associations; Cooperatives; Guilds
Crafts business
  bookkeeping system in, 133-134, 138
  forms for, 135-137
  components of, 4-6
  as corporation, 147-149
  efficiency in, 29, 30, 36
  employees of, 71-72, 156-158
  individual approach to, 7-8, 10, 19, 22
  insurance in, 152-155
  laws relating to, 131-132, 150-152
  learning of, 158-159
  partnership in, 145-147
  pension plans for, 155-156
  profits of, 6
  sole proprietorship of, 145
  taxation of, 138-145
  See also Craft shop; *specific subjects*
Crafts buyers. *See* Customers
Crafts courses, guides to, 103
Crafts Horizon, 171
Crafts magazines, 12
  list of, 176-181
  as resource, 173-174
  See also Magazines
Craftspeople
  business sense of, 3-4, 30
  earnings of, 6
  government assistance for, 172-173
  job opportunities for, 99-117
  in mail order, 98
  needs of, 7-9, 22

volume *vs* self expression and, 6-7, 9, 11
Crafts shops
  guides to, 39
  starting of
    financing in, 114-115
    inventory in, 117
    location of, 115-116
    training for, 113-114
  See also Crafts business; Stores
Crafts shows
  benefits of, 54-55
  demonstrations in, 55
  display units at, 59-60, 61
  drawbacks of, 61-62
  financial records of, 57
  guides to, 50
  seasons for, 58
  security at, 60-61
  selection of, 51-52, 53, 61
  selling at, 55-57
  supplies for, 58-59
  types of, 50-54, 62
Crafts supply stores, instructors in, 100-101
Customers
  categories of, 16
  market research on, 17-18
Customers' profile, 15-18
Custom orders, pricing of, 22

Davis, Mary Kay, 108, 109
Declining-balance method, in depreciation claims, 140
Deductible expenses, 138-139, 141-142
  and depreciation, 140-141
Defect lawsuits, 154
Demonstrations, in craft shows, 55
Department stores, direct sales to, 44
Depreciation claims, methods of, 140-141
Design
  of business cards, 125-126
  in direct mail sales, 74
  fads in, 14
  importance of, 5-6, 18, 20
  of kits, 88-89, 109
  of labels, 126-127
  marketability *vs* originality in, 12
  market research for, 13-14, 15-18
  popular sellers in, 34
  professional consultation in, 18
Design costs, calculation of, 29

Design integrity, 14
Design jobs
  on freelance basis, 109-110
  in house, 110
Design patent, 151
Design reproduction, 6-7
  discipline for, 9, 21
  and pricing, 22
Direct mail sales
  through advertising media, 77-82
  benefits of, 73
  brochure in, 77-78
  catalog in, 83-88
  government regulation of, 90-91
  guidelines for, 74
  of kits, 88-90
  mailing lists for, 74-77
  packing in, 92-94
  shipping of, 92, 94-96
  thirty-day-delivery in, 82, 90
Disability insurance, 154-155
Discounts, for wholesale buyers, 35
Discriminating buyers, of crafts, 16, 17
Display ads, in direct mail sales, 74-75
Display units, at crafts shows, 59-60, 61

Employees, of crafts business, 71-72,
  156-158
Employer identification number, 156
Employment. *See* Job opportunities
Entertainment expenses, deductions for,
  141
Express mail, 96

Fads, in craft design, 14
Farmers'   Home   Administration
  (USDA), and rural craft co-ops,
  166
Feel Free (Viscott), 9
Filing system, 133, 137
Fine arts floater, to property insurance,
  153
Fixed assets, defined, 134
Flea markets, 112-113
Flyers
  distribution of, 127-128
  production of, 128
Food and Drug Administration (FDA),
  regulations of, 91
Fringe benefits, 157

Galleries
  consignment selling in

benefits of, 44-45
contract for, 47
interview for, 46
Gifts, in direct mail sales. 74
Goodfellow Catalog of Wonderfull
  Things, 84-85
Government
  direct mail regulations of, 90-91
  writing for, 109
Government aid
  to cooperatives, 166-167
  to craftspeople, 172-173
Guilds, 169-170, 172

Handbill. *See* Flyer
Health insurance, 155
Home office
  overhead in, 31
  selling in, 111-112, 132
  tax deductions on, 139

Indigenous population, of craft buyers,
  16-17
Insurance, types of, 152-155
Intangible assets, defined, 134
Invoices, information on, 136
IRS, tax guidance from, 142-143

Job opportunities, in craft-related fields,
  99-117
Juried craft shows, 52-53

Kits
  advertising of, 89-90
  design and construction of, 88-89, 109

Labels
  design of, 126-127
  for handling, 154
  for mail orders, 92
  personalization of, 19
Labor costs
  calculation of, 25, 28-30
  reduction of, 33
Lecturing, 104-106
  self promotion through, 129
Liabilities, defined, 134
Liability insurance, 153-154
Limited partnerships, 147
Liquid assets, defined, 134

Magazines
  advertising in, 79-82

guides to, 80
writing for, 106-108
See also Crafts magazines
Mailing lists
compilation of 75-76
refining of, 76-77
Mail order sales. *See* Direct mail sales
Market research
and design, 13-14
customer profile in, 15-18
Materials
buying of, 27
cost calculation of, 25-27
cost cutting in, 33
regional use of, 9
Medical coverage, 155
Modern Packaging Encyclopedia, 94
Museum of Contemporary Crafts, 172
Museums
craft related jobs in, 104
shops in, 47-48

National Endowment for the Arts,
grants of, 172
Newspaper advertising, in direct mail
sales, 78-82
Newspapers, publicity in, 119-121

One-person show, 62
Open crafts shows, 52
Overhead costs, calculation of, 30-31

Packaging, promotion through, 127
Packing
boxing in, 93-94
labeling in, 92
materials for, 93
Packing and Shipping of Crafts, 94
Packing slip, use of, 135-136
Parcel post, 95
Partnership
agreements in, 147
and financial status, 146
Patent protection, 151
Pension plans, 155
Photographing Crafts (Barsness), 123
Photography
mailing of, 124
in promotion campaigns, 122-124
Press releases
format of, 120-121
photography in, 124
Price range, establishment of, 5-6, 21-24

Pricing
for catalog sales, 84
cost calculation in, 25-32
for crafts shows, 57-58
in direct sales, 34-35
formula for, 32-33
importance of, 5
for mail orders, 74
Product flyers, uses of, 68-69
Productivity
estimation of, 30
and profit, 33-34, 36
Product liability insurance, 153-154
Product promoters, 72
Profit, 6
calculation of, 25, 31-32
in craft shows, 53
and productivity, 33-34, 36
taxation of, 143
Promotional fee, 72
Promotion campaigns
business cards in, 125-126
flyers in, 127-128
labels in, 126-127
mailers in, 122
packaging in, 127
photography for, 122-125
Property insurance, fine arts floater to,
153
Publicity
news angles for, 118-122
sources of, 128-130
Public liability insurance, 153
Purchase order form, use of, 135
Purloining, of samples, 70-71

Quality, importance of, 18-19

Radio publicity, 121-122
Retailing. *See* Selling
Retail stores. *See* Stores

Sales employees, hiring of, 71-72
Sales representatives
contract with, 65-66
selection of, 64
uses of, 63-64
working with, 66-67
Sales tax, 57
for mail orders, 91
Sample makers, 110
Samples, purloining of, 70-71
Schedule C, 142

Self-employment income, taxation of, 143
Selling
  on consignment, 37-48
  through cooperatives, 163
  at crafts shows, 55-57
  factors in
    design, 18, 20
    materials, 19
    personal interest, 19
    workmanship, 18-19
  in owner's store, 113-117
  through product promoters, 72
  in public markets, 112
  to retail stores, 68-71
  through sales employees, 71-72, 156-158
  through sales representatives, 63-67
  seasonal sales in, 48
  from studios, 113
  through wholesale distributors, 71
  See also Direct mail sales
Selling expenses, calculation of, 32
Selling price. *See* Price range, Pricing
Shipping methods, 92, 94-98
Shopping centers, as store location, 116
Shops. *See* Craft shops; Stores
Small Business Administration, 117, 158
Southern Highland Handicraft Guild, 169-170
Special delivery service, 95
Standard Periodical Directory, 80
State governments, arts councils of, 173
Statement, use of, 136-137
Stores
    for consignment selling
      contract with, 41-43
      guides to, 39
      selection of, 38, 39-40
    direct sales to, 43-44, 68-71
    filling orders to, 67
    See also Crafts shops
Straight-line method, in depreciation claims, 140
Studio, lecture/demonstration in, 129-130
Sub Chapter "S" corporation, 148

Tangible assets, defined, 134
Taxation
  assistance with, 142-143
  on corporations, 148
  deductible expenses in, 138-142

guides to, 142
late payment of, 144-145
of partnerships, 147
of profit, 143
on self-employment income, 143-144
Teaching
  in apprenticeship programs, 102-103
  in colleges and universities, 103
  in community centers, 100
  in craft stores, 100-101
  guides to, 103
  in private classes, 101-102
  promotion through, 129
Television publicity, 121-122
Thirty-day-delivery, for mail orders, 82, 90
Thomas' Register of Manufacturers, 110
Tourists, as crafts buyers, 17
Trade discounts, 35
Trademark, filing for, 151-152
Trade shows, 54
Trading up, 35
Travel expenses, deductions for, 141-142

United Parcel Service (UPS), shipping by, 96-97
US Census Bureau, list of business/population figures of, 115-116
US Post Office, shipping by, 94-96, 97

Viscott, David, 9
Volume work
  discipline for, 9, 21-22
  pricing of, 22, 23

Weaver, Peter, 9
Wholesale distributors, selling through, 71
Wholesale shows, 54
Wholesale price
  formula for, 32-33
  overhead in, 31
Writers' Digest Magazine, 106-107
Writer's Market, 80-81, 106
Writing
  article proposals in, 107-108
  book presentations in, 108
  collaboration in, 109
  for government, 109
  markets for, 106-107

You, Inc. (Weaver), 9